FOLLOW GOD - DEVOTIONAL

Published by - Spines
ISBN: 979-8-89569-151-9

FOLLOW GOD - DEVOTIONAL

JENNIFER ANDERSON

Day 1

Hebrews 12:1 NOG

Since we are surrounded by so many examples of faith, we must get rid of everything that slows us down, especially sin that distracts us. We must run the race that lies ahead of us and never give up.

Why hold on to what God desires you to release? If He desires you to release it, it will not serve you in this season He is bringing you into. If God's not in it, why are you?

Personal Reflection: What is God saying to Me?

Day 2

Matthew 6:14–15 NKJV

For if you forgive men their trespasses, your heavenly Father will also forgive you. But if you do not forgive men their trespasses, neither will your Father forgive your trespasses.

Let any thoughts of Christians who fall into sin move you to justice, empathy, compassion, and forgiveness. Remember David—king of many, sinned greatly with Bathsheba, set up and murdered her husband, moved her in, had a child—but God. Justice served, ultimately forgiven. Given another son whom God loved and blessed greatly. Ask God to help move you to forgiveness.

Personal Reflection: What is God saying to Me?

Colossians 3:13 NIRV

Put up with one another. Forgive one another if you are holding something against someone. Forgive just as the Lord forgave you.

I asked the Lord for help as my tolerance to receive others as they are has diminished. I want people to conform and serve me. I have become self-absorbed in conversations. God says this is self-worship and control—Satan, and to use the magnitude of His energy and presence in me to love.

Personal Reflection: What is God saying to Me?

Day 4

2 Corinthians 3:18 KJV

But we all, with open face beholding as in a glass the glory of the Lord, are changed into the same image from glory to glory, even as by the Spirit of the Lord.

God desires you to progress. He doesn't want you to remain where you are. He wants you to move on to the next stage of elevation in who He has called you to become and what He desires you to do. Have you gotten comfortable where God has you?

Personal Reflection: What is God saying to Me?

Day 5

Psalm 139:15-16 NIV

My frame was not hidden from you when I was made in the secret place.

After being saved, I was always frustrated, angry, in a rush, and irritable. I tried everything I could think of, but nothing worked—only surrender. God had to do a deep work in me to help me work through negative thought patterns, spiritual warfare, trauma, self-worth, and deliverance. Invite Him in to help you too.

Personal Reflection: What is God saying to Me?

Day 6

Exodus 4:10-15

Then Moses said to the Lord, "Please, Lord, I have never been eloquent, neither recently nor in time past, nor since You have spoken to Your servant; for I am slow of speech and slow of tongue." The Lord said to him, "Who has made man's mouth? Or who makes him mute or deaf, or seeing or blind? Is it not I, the Lord? Now then go, and I, even I, will be with your mouth, and teach you what you are to say." But he said, "Please, Lord, now send the message by whomever You will."

Aaron to Be Moses' Mouthpiece

Then the anger of the Lord burned against Moses, and He said, "Is there not your brother Aaron the Levite? I know that he speaks fluently. And moreover, behold, he is coming out to meet you; when he sees you, he will be glad in his heart. You are to speak to him and put the words in his mouth; and I, even I, will be with your mouth and his mouth, and I will teach you what you are to do."

Moses felt inadequate to be used in God's grand plan to free His people from slavery. This did not change God's mind. God worked with Moses to free His people and stayed with Moses, leading and guiding along the way. It was never about Moses's capability but God's. Trust Him.

Personal Reflection: What is God saying to Me?

Psalm 37:23–24 KJV

The steps of a good man are ordered by the LORD: And he delighteth in his way. Though he fall, he shall not be utterly cast down: For the LORD upholdeth him with his hand.

God deals with people in steps. He wants you to take the step you know to take, then He will reveal the next one. Intimacy, purpose, identity, and relationship finances are all interrelated and will bloom over time. His steps are not out of order but by His order. Trust them.

Personal Reflection: What is God saying to Me?

Day 8

Matthew 16:24-26 DLNT

Deny Yourself, Take Up Your Cross, And Follow Me. Some Here Will See Me In My Kingdom.

Then Jesus said to His disciples, "If anyone wants to come after Me, let him deny himself, take up his cross, and follow Me. For whoever wants to save his life will lose it. But whoever loses his life for My sake will find it. For what will a person be profited if he gains the whole world but forfeits his life? Or what will a person give in exchange for his life?"

What are your excuses? You don't have time, money, or know-how? Ask yourself if you really want to serve God? If so, you'll find a way. 2 a.m. is for those seeking, disciplined, and determined for what they want. Desire. Decide. Commit. Pursue. Make a way.

Personal Reflection: What is God saying to Me?

Day 9

1 Samuel 15:22 NLT

But Samuel replied, "What is more pleasing to the Lord: your burnt offerings and sacrifices or your obedience to His voice? Listen! Obedience is better than sacrifice, and submission is better than offering the fat of rams."

Better than your idea of "amazing" is obedient. You may be waiting to do something God has called you to do because you are waiting for the resources so it can be amazing. Don't sit on God's instruction. Don't wait in disobedience for perfection. If God's asking, simply obey.

Personal Reflection: What is God saying to Me?

Day 10

Psalm 55:22 NLT

Give your burdens to the LORD, and He will take care of you. He will not permit the godly to slip and fall.

Stop carrying weight that doesn't belong to you. Some of you are in relationships that don't serve you, in roles you gave to yourself that are not required, and engage in activities that are unnecessary. Know these things are hindering you from progress in and with God. Let them go.

Personal Reflection: What is God saying to Me?

DAY 11

Isaiah 43:19 AMP

Listen carefully, I am about to do a new thing. Now it will spring forth; Will you not be aware of it?

I believe the church is changing. The four walls will no longer stand. The old will fall away. I believe that God is birthing a new church online and in homes. He will teach people how to know Him intimately, seek Him, explore spiritual giftings, and build new churches.

Personal Reflection: What is God saying to Me?

Day 12

1 Timothy 4:12 NIV

Don't let anyone look down on you. Don't let anyone look down on you because you are young, but set an example for the believers in speech, in conduct, in love, in faith, and in purity.

Just for laughs. Have you ever had someone pray for you or heard from someone else that someone's praying for you and it's all real suspect? "Like, I'm good. What you tryna say? Don't pray for me; how about I pray for you!!" Oh Jesus work on our hearts. Forgive us.

Personal Reflection: What is God saying to Me?

Day 13

Matthew 25:23 NIV

His master replied, "Well done, good and faithful servant! You have been faithful with a few things; I will put you in charge of many things. Come and share your master's happiness!"

How do you measure success? Regardless of what time you rise or fall, are you living for God? See, success is measured by your obedience to God not by worldly markers of material possessions, money, status, power, or vanity. That is living for Satan.

Personal Reflection: What is God saying to Me?

Day 14

1 Corinthians 1:27 KJV

But God hath chosen the foolish things of the world to confound the wise.

Losing my religion was tough. God sent me through a season where He led me to secular music, a worldly appearance, and withdrawal from traditional devotion time. I often told God it wasn't spiritual. He wanted to remove the rules that created a prison for me and limited me.

Personal Reflection: What is God saying to Me?

Matthew 17:17 NCV

Jesus answered, "You people have no faith, and your lives are all wrong. How long must I put up with you? How long must I continue to be patient with you? Bring the boy here."

What is your Christian pet peeve? Mine is when people invite me into a conversation and ask me to pray for someone. This person was led to pray. Why don't they pray? What is wrong with their lips? See, I like to pray in love and get to know people and the needs of the moment. Irks me.

Personal Reflection: What is God saying to Me?

Day 16

Matthew 11:28-30 MSG

Burned out on religion? Come to me. Get away with me and you'll recover your life. I'll show you how to take a real rest.

Decide to go away with God. Go as far as God will take you. Leave all that you know religion, tradition, Christianity and God behind and let God reveal to you who He is and who you are in Him. Oh, get lost in Him. Decide to go all the way.

Personal Reflection: What is God saying to Me?

DAY 17

Proverbs 8:17 ESV

I love those who love me, and those who seek me diligently find me.

You want to follow God but don't hear His voice? Seek God with everything you have. Seek Him early and then all day. Do what you know you need to do now. Continue to seek Him diligently. He will meet you there and your communication and relationship will evolve.

Personal Reflection: What is God saying to Me?

Day 18

Romans 8:14 NIV

For those who are led by the Spirit of God are the children of God.

Take God with you. Don't leave God in your prayer closet, at home, at church. Take Him with you all day long. He wants to order your steps and live life with you. He wants to lead and guide you in all truth. Let God live in *and* with you. Allow Him to experience life with you.

Personal Reflection: What is God saying to Me?

DAY 19

John 8:12 NIV

When Jesus spoke again to the people, he said, "I am the light of the world. Whoever follows me will never walk in darkness, but will have the light of life."

I went through a challenging time. God showed me that He wanted to see what I would do in the dark. Would I give up, turn back or still strive to get to Him? I did it all for a short time then leaned into God with all I had. I ended up chasing the light.

Personal Reflection: What is God saying to Me?

1 Samuel 16:14 EHV

The Spirit of the Lord departed from Saul, and an evil spirit from the Lord tormented him.

2 Timothy 1:7 CEV

God's Spirit doesn't make cowards out of us. The Spirit gives us power, love, and self-control.

Confusion, disorientation, pressure are used as tools to see what one does at their worst. God will allow you to be afflicted in this way to see when you are at your worst, what you do. In this time, cling to God and know power, love and a sound mind is on the way.

Personal Reflection: What is God saying to Me?

DAY 21

John 1:38 NIV

Turning around, Jesus saw them following and asked, "What do you want?" They said, "Rabbi" (which means "Teacher"), "where are you staying?"

What do you want from God? It will show up in your everyday life. Evaluate your daily schedule and overall life. Does it look like someone who wants nothing to do with Jesus, who wants just activity or who went only so far but settled? Let your daily life look like one who wants to go all the way with Jesus.

Personal Reflection: What is God saying to Me?

Luke 2:49 NKJV

And He said to them, "Why did you seek Me? Did you not know that I must be about My Father's business?"

Talk to Jesus first. In this season I thought, if you want me to do something you would be better off talking to Jesus first. I don't have to listen to you or do what you ask, but I do need to do what "thus sayeth the Lord". Be known for your obedience to Jesus.

Personal Reflection: What is God saying to Me?

Day 23

Exodus 34:14 NIV

Do not worship any other god, for the LORD, whose name is Jealous, is a jealous God.

Just as we have a jealous God, Satan gets jealous too. Now you are talking to God, being used of God, submitted to God, following God and leaning into all things God. He is looking for ways to get into your ministry and relationship with God. He lost you but is looking for a way back in.

Personal Reflection: What is God saying to Me?

Day 24

Ephesians 2:10 ESV

For we are His workmanship, created in Christ Jesus for good works, which God prepared beforehand, that we should walk in them.

I thought there was a difference between actual self and life vs. Christian self and life. At church, around Christians or people I've ministered to, I donned my Christian persona. At home, work, etc., I was someone else. I matured when Christ revealed my true identity, and I walked in that 24/7.

Personal Reflection: What is God saying to Me?

Day 25

Colossians 2:20-23 NIV

Since you died with Christ to the elemental spiritual forces of this world, why, as though you still belonged to the world, do you submit to its rules: "Do not handle! Do not taste! Do not touch!"? These rules, which have to do with things that are all destined to perish with use, are based on merely human commands and teachings. Such regulations indeed have an appearance of wisdom, with their self-imposed worship, their false humility and their harsh treatment of the body, but they lack any value in restraining sensual indulgence.

Live in the grace and truth of Jesus Christ. Through Moses, the law came. Even grace was built in the law—a foreshadowing of Christ. If they broke it, there was action to take. Paul asks us why live under rule when we are free. Do not sin but know that you are free. Don't let anyone or anything keep you bound.

Personal Reflection: What is God saying to Me?

John 15:18 NIV

If the world hates you, keep in mind that it hated Me first.

Stop changing so they will like you. They will hate you because they hated Christ, and He was sinless. He only did what He saw the Father doing, and they crucified Him. It's not you. It's them. Stay you in Christ, boo.

Personal Reflection: What is God saying to Me?

1 Peter 5:6–7 MSG

So be content with who you are, and don't put on airs. God's strong hand is on you; He'll promote you at the right time. Live carefree before God; He is most careful with you. Don't touch their filthy things, and I will welcome you.

Know that many of you are set apart. Stop trying to adjust yourself so that you can fit into the group and be accepted—whether it be a job, family, or even church. You will never fit in because you are set apart. Stop trying. Be who God has called you to be.

Personal Reflection: What is God saying to Me?

2 Timothy 3:1-5 MSG

Don't be naive. There are difficult times ahead. As the end approaches, people are going to be self-absorbed, money-hungry, self-promoting, stuck-up, profane, contemptuous of parents, crude, coarse, dog-eat-dog, unbending, slanderers, impulsively wild, savage, cynical, treacherous, ruthless, bloated windbags, addicted to lust, and allergic to God. They'll make a show of religion, but behind the scenes they're animals. Stay clear of these people.

Have nothing to do with lawless people. 2 Timothy lets us know what the heart and actions of men will be in end of days. It says HAVE NOTHING TO DO WITH THESE PEOPLE. Do not feel guilty about distancing yourself or ending relationships with these types of people.

Personal Reflection: What is God saying to Me?

DAY 29

Romans 5:3-5 NIV

Not only so, but we also glory in our sufferings, because we know that suffering produces perseverance; perseverance, character; and character, hope.

Sin and gym comparison. In the gym we don't like comfort. We look for resistance. We challenge ourselves with increasing intensity. We know through struggle and the breaking down, growth will take place. View your walk the same way. Sin exposes your heart; resist and grow through it.

Personal Reflection: What is God saying to Me?

Day 30

John 14:6 NIV

Jesus answered, "I am the way and the truth and the life. No one comes to the Father except through me."

Stop the "Jesus and" movement. Jesus and fitness, coffee. Nothing should be elevated to the position of Christ. You have made a thing an idol. Jesus requires nothing. He is enough. Jesus is the way, the truth, and the life. Nothing else. Jesus is the way to salvation, life. Repent if you have a "Jesus and" mindset.

Personal Reflection: What is God saying to Me?

DAY 31

1 Corinthians 3:2–3 NLT

I had to feed you with milk, not with solid food, because you weren't ready for anything stronger. And you still aren't ready, for you are still controlled by your sinful nature. You are jealous of one another and quarrel with each other.

Getting off milk onto solid food. Do you want to? Or are you content with your spiritual walk? Are you comfortable? Seek more depth in Jesus. Ascend higher in His ways and thoughts. Many should be teaching but are comfortable receiving. Challenge yourself to move into the more.

Personal Reflection: What is God saying to Me?

Day 32

Romans 7:14-17 NLT

So the trouble is not with the law, for it is spiritual and good. The trouble is with me, for I am all too human, a slave to sin. I don't really understand myself, for I want to do what is right, but I don't do it. Instead, I do what I hate. But if I know that what I am doing is wrong, this shows that I agree that the law is good. So I am not the one doing wrong; it is sin living in me that does it.

If you are struggling with sin in your Christian walk, know that even Paul struggled, and he wrote most of the New Testament and referred to himself as a prisoner of Christ. Romans 7:15 lets us peek into the struggle Paul had as he did what he hated but loved good. We all fall short of the glory, and none of us have arrived. Repent, seek forgiveness, press forward.

Personal Reflection: What is God saying to Me?

DAY 33

2 Corinthians 5:20 ESV

Therefore, we are ambassadors for Christ, God making His appeal through us. We implore you on behalf of Christ: be reconciled to God.

In giving wisdom, Christian, know that many are coming to you to hear the voice of God whether directly or through your interpretation of Him based on your overall Christian experience. You are an ambassador of God. Always seek God's words or redirect them to God.

Personal Reflection: What is God saying to Me?

Luke 22:31-32 NLT

Simon, Simon, Satan has asked to sift each of you like wheat. But I have pleaded in prayer for you, Simon, that your faith should not fail. So when you have repented and turned to me again, strengthen your brothers.

We all suffer, struggle, and are tempted. Know that whatever you are going through, no matter what stage of Christianity you are in—from baby to mature—we are all challenged. Do not feel unworthy or alone. Give it over to God and let Him make you strong. Then go strengthen your brother.

Personal Reflection: What is God saying to Me?

DAY 35

Matthew 6:24 NIV

No one can serve two masters. Either you will hate the one and love the other, or you will be devoted to the one and despise the other. You cannot serve both God and money.

Don't pursue wealth over anointing. Consider when you get wealthy, what will you do with it? I want God's anointing on me so everything I touch with that money will be of Him and used for His glory. I don't want wealth to consume me. I want to use it for kingdom building. God let the money come with You.

Personal Reflection: What is God saying to Me?

Day 36

Matthew 10:14 AMP

Whoever does not welcome you, nor listen to your message, as you leave that house or city, shake the dust [of it] off your feet [in contempt, breaking all ties].

Don't overstay your time at a place or with a person because on paper it seems like the right thing. Trust the stirring to consider leaving. Bring that to God. God *will* have you leave brothers, mothers, children, wives, churches, jobs, and ministries if it does not serve His will for you.

Personal Reflection: What is God saying to Me?

Day 37

Hebrews 6:17-18

So, when God desired to show more convincingly to the heirs of the promise the unchangeable character of His purpose, He guaranteed it with an oath, so that by two unchangeable things, in which it is impossible for God to lie.

Feeling like God lied to you? Oftentimes, God will communicate a thing to you and when it doesn't come as expected, you get mad and think God lied. No, it simply happened in a way that you may not be able to detect and not as imagined. This is a tool to test and reveal the heart of His children. Will you leave or stay? Did you want God or the thing?

Personal Reflection: What is God saying to Me?

DAY 38

Romans 12:12 ESV

Rejoice in hope, be patient in tribulation, be constant in prayer.

Lighten up, chosen ones. Yes, it's hard. It's difficult. You have been through things you can't even discuss. You are tired and worn out. Decide you will not wallow in sorrow and despair. Muster up the strength one more time to keep going and find joy and laughter.

Personal Reflection: What is God saying to Me?

Proverbs 10:9 ESV

Whoever walks in integrity walks securely, but he who makes his ways crooked will be found out.

Again, tell yourself the truth. You don't like them. They are mean. You hate the church you go to. You don't like the job. You don't want to be a (_) anymore. Then give that over to God so He can give you strategy for it. Don't live in denial or fakeness. Face it, ask God to help you.

Personal Reflection: What is God saying to Me?

Day 40

John 14:15 NIRV

If you love Me, you will obey what I command.

The moment is now. Do it. Get in God's flow. Do what He asked you to do. His time is now! God's anointing, grace, and favor is on the now moment of obedience. Don't wait and leave God to when you are ready. Relinquish control and learn to dance with God.

Personal Reflection: What is God saying to Me?

Psalm 30:5 NIV

For his anger lasts only a moment, but his favor lasts a lifetime; weeping may stay for the night, but rejoicing comes in the morning.

God tells me I need to give up the "woe is me" attitude. What He put me through was beautifully rough, but I've had enough time to rest, sulk, recover, reestablish, and now it's time to get moving. It was by His authority, for His purpose, and for my ultimate good. He wants me to seek joy, curiosity, and obedience again.

Personal Reflection: What is God saying to Me?

Day 42

Luke 5:16 GNT

But he would go away to lonely places where he prayed.

Living in isolation is tough. I spoke to God about not being able to speak to anybody about the amazing world I've been pulled into with the Lord and all that He is doing with me. He told me to embrace my unique and special odyssey and leave what is old and common behind.

Personal Reflection: What is God saying to Me?

Luke 14:26-27 NLT

If you want to be my disciple, you must, by comparison, hate everyone else—your father and mother, wife and children, brothers and sisters—yes, even your own life. Otherwise, you cannot be my disciple. And if you do not carry your own cross and follow me, you cannot be my disciple.

I asked God why we are not living as disciples, fulfilling the Great Commission, and doing greater works than Jesus. He said, "Because many are not my disciples. They are merely bearing my name but not coming after Me. They also strive to not know or become love. I am love. They deny love—the receiving and the giving. They deny Me."

Personal Reflection: What is God saying to Me?

Day 44

Matthew 28:18-20 NIV

Then Jesus came to them and said, "All authority in heaven and on earth has been given to me. Therefore go and make disciples of all nations, baptizing them in the name of the Father and of the Son and of the Holy Spirit, and teaching them to obey everything I have commanded you. And surely I am with you always, to the very end of the age."

Our great commission as disciples of Christ is to go out and make disciples of all nations. We are to teach, baptize, heal the sick, raise the dead, and cast out demons. Has this been your Christian experience? Are you a disciple? Ask Jesus to help you fulfill His commission.

Personal Reflection: What is God saying to Me?

DAY 45

Luke 1:37 ESV

For nothing will be impossible with God.

Are you stressing? Where is your faith? As long as you are seeking God's will and following Him, you are doing all you can. Whatever happens, good or bad, will work out for your good. Simply trust Him. He knows your limitations and can guide, even course-correct, without your awareness.

Personal Reflection: What is God saying to Me?

Matthew 16:4 CEV

You want a sign because you are evil and won't believe! But the only sign you will be given is what happened to Jonah. Then Jesus left.

I asked God, "Is it wrong for me to seek miracles, signs, and wonders?" He told me it was wrong to simply desire to see them as a form of entertainment or as proof of His existence. I should desire to want people liberated from what afflicts them and to be used to do so.

Personal Reflection: What is God saying to Me?

Day 47

Psalms 51:10–12 TPT

Keep creating in me a clean heart. Fill me with pure thoughts and holy desires, ready to please you. May you never reject me! May you never take from me your sacred Spirit! Let my passion for life be restored, tasting joy in every breakthrough you bring to me. Hold me close to you with a willing spirit that obeys whatever you say.

Ezekiel 36:25-27 NLT

Then I will sprinkle clean water on you, and you will be clean. Your filth will be washed away, and you will no longer worship idols. And I will give you a new heart, and I will put a new spirit in you. I will take out your stony, stubborn heart and give you a tender, responsive heart. And I will put my Spirit in you so that you will follow my decrees and be careful to obey my regulations.

I prayed for us to have a clean heart according to Psalms 51 and Ezekiel 36. God, please renew a right spirit in us, restore to us the joy of Your salvation, and uphold us with a willing spirit. Sprinkle us with water, cleanse us of our idols. Help us, Lord. Cause us to walk in your ways.

Personal Reflection: What is God saying to Me?

Day 48

Ephesians 4:22-24 ESV

To put off your old self, which belongs to your former manner of life and is corrupt through deceitful desires, and to be renewed in the spirit of your minds, and to put on the new self, created after the likeness of God in true righteousness and holiness.

Do you want a new life? Let us be honest with ourselves. The new life we are praying for requires letting go of the old life. Are you willing to give up your habits, ways, or understanding for God's? If not, bring your truth to Him so He can help you release what is no longer required.

Personal Reflection: What is God saying to Me?

Matthew 6:6-7 KJV

But thou, when thou prayest, enter into thy closet, and when thou hast shut thy door, pray to thy Father which is in secret; and thy Father which seeth in secret shall reward thee openly.

I added more to my prayer closet. Whatever we need to do or even desire to do to seek God diligently will do nothing but reap great rewards. Find new and fresh ways to meet with God. Don't let your walk with Christ grow stale or drift from God. Pursue Him any way you can.

Personal Reflection: What is God saying to Me?

Day 50

2 Corinthians 1:20 NKJV

For all the promises of God in Him are "Yes," and in Him "Amen," to the glory of God through us.

My belief fuels me. I believe in God. I know He is real just as I know I'm real. I believe in the promises He has for me and what He has planned for me. I believe He loves me and is for me. I am able to keep going because He brings me back to this belief. Do you believe?

Personal Reflection: What is God saying to Me?

Day 51

Proverbs 3:5-6 NIV

Trust in the LORD with all your heart and lean not on your own understanding; in all your ways submit to Him, and He will make your paths straight.

What will it take for you to blindly follow God? He desires you to move in step with Him. He wants you to learn to dance with Him. God is the best dancer and wants to put you on display so people can see you dance greatly with Him and then they will seek to dance with Him as well.

Personal Reflection: What is God saying to Me?

Matthew 20:22 BSB

"What do you want?" he inquired. She answered, "Declare that in your kingdom one of these two sons of mine may sit at your right hand, and the other at your left." "You do not know what you are asking," Jesus replied. "Can you drink the cup I am going to drink?"

Don't seek to have someone else's spiritual walk or anointing. Let it only inspire you to seek your own walk with God. Invite Him to meet you where you are and draw you unto Himself, walking you to where He wants you to go so you can handle and withstand the weight of heavy anointings.

Personal Reflection: What is God saying to Me?

Day 53

Ephesians 2:10 BSB

For we are God's workmanship, created in Christ Jesus to do good works, which God prepared in advance as our way of life.

The work God has called you to do would be so much easier if you just turned it over to God. Let Him dictate what you do and how you do it. Jesus was about His Father's business, and they hated and crucified Him. Be obedient and let the chips fall where they may.

Personal Reflection: What is God saying to Me?

2 Corinthians 12:9–10 NKJV

And He said to me, "My grace is sufficient for you, for My strength is made perfect in weakness." Therefore most gladly will rather boast in my infirmities.

I told God I was tired of hard. I didn't want to suffer anymore. I admitted that I was weak. He said that He led me to this point so that I can finally surrender to Him and operate out of His strength and not my own. His strength and glory would be revealed through my weakness.

Personal Reflection: What is God saying to Me?

Job 23:10 NCV

But God knows the way that I take, and when He has tested me, I will come out like gold.

When God is the one you love and give all to, but also is the one allowing hardship and discomfort, it can feel abusive. The world would tell you to leave. As Jesus had trouble processing, asking the Father, "Why have you forsaken me," He offers the answer. Accept God's will over your own. Don't jump off the cross.

Personal Reflection: What is God saying to Me?

Day 56

Proverbs 16:4 NRSV

The LORD has made everything for its purpose, even the wicked for the day of trouble.

I asked God how I operate with Him exposing me to worldly things. He responded that He created all and will use even the wicked things in days of trouble. Those things had no power over Him and He was in me. Therefore, they had no power over me. I needed to be amongst them and their worldliness so that I could be used to save them.

Personal Reflection: What is God saying to Me?

Matthew 7:13-14 ESV

Enter by the narrow gate. For the gate is wide and the way is easy that leads to destruction, and those who enter by it are many. For the gate is narrow and the way is hard that leads to life, and those who find it are few.

Do not choose the easy way out. God wants you in the HARD because this is the way. Don't you know He can make the seemingly easy hard and the hard easy; or can keep the easy easy so you grow tired of it or the hard hard so you grow? Choose not hard or easy, choose God's will.

Personal Reflection: What is God saying to Me?

Proverbs 11:30 ESV

The fruit of the righteous is a tree of life, and whoever captures souls is wise.

In the military, I understood that lives were on the line and the future generation of the military depended on my actions. My life mattered only up to a point because if the greater good required that life, it would be taken. Know, in our Christian walks, souls are on the line. Get over your feelings.

Personal Reflection: What is God saying to Me?

Romans 12:1 ESV

I appeal to you therefore, brothers, by the mercies of God, to present your bodies as a living sacrifice, holy and acceptable to God, which is your spiritual worship.

What the military taught me, which was crucial for my walk with Christ, was that my feelings didn't matter. When I signed, I forfeited my life to the military. Each day I had an appointed place of duty and needed to show up a specific way because there was something bigger than me at stake. You have given your very body over to Christ. There is an appointed time for you to get to the place God desires, and you must be ready to withstand the weight and magnitude of it. You must be prepared. Many are tied to your obedience. Obey.

Personal Reflection: What is God saying to Me?

Day 60

Ezekiel 4:12–17 ERV

"You must make your bread each day. You must get dry human dung and burn it. Then you must cook the bread over this burning dung. You must eat this bread in front of the people." Then the LORD said, "This will show that the family of Israel will eat unclean bread in foreign countries and that I am the one who forced them to leave Israel and go to those countries!"

Then I said, "Oh, but Lord GOD, I have never eaten any unclean food. I have never eaten meat from an animal that died from a disease or from an animal that was killed by a wild animal. I have never eaten unclean meat—not from the time that I was a little baby until now. None of that bad meat ever entered my mouth." Then God said to me, "Very well, I will let you use dry cow dung to cook your bread. You don't have to use dry human dung."

It's not about what you can't do. What can you do? Work with God. He would rather you talk to Him about all that you struggle with as He calls you into extraordinary things beyond yourself than to run from Him. He may create baby steps for you to do the hard thing. Go to Him. He'll make a way.

Personal Reflection: What is God saying to Me?

Romans 8:7 ASV

Because the mind of the flesh is enmity against God; for it is not subject to the law of God, neither indeed can it be:

Fight to get to Jesus. Is it hard to do anything relating to God? Know, this is not just life or you. Something is preventing you from seeking God. The flesh is disinterested in hanging out with its enemy. There is a death match that must take place. Decide to crucify the flesh. Subdue what is hostile to God and find yourself free to go to Him.

Personal Reflection: What is God saying to Me?

DAY 62

John 10:10 NIV

The thief comes only to steal and kill and destroy; I have come that they may have life and have it to the full.

What is Satan's agenda? He wants you dead. He wants to kill, steal, destroy, and devour by your very own hands. Consider how much Satan hates you to want you to commit suicide, separate you from God and have your soul, torment you and cause death and destruction in your life. What is your strategy against that? He will not respond to you, only the authority of Jesus Christ. Invite Jesus in. Abide in Him and Him in you.

Personal Reflection: What is God saying to Me?

1 Peter 5:8 NIV

Be alert and of sober mind. Your enemy, the devil, prowls around like a roaring lion, looking for someone to devour.

Why you out here unprotected, outside the covering of God? God wants your whole soul, but so does Satan. He is after you killing, stealing, destroying, devouring, and lying to you and all attached. If he is not, you should be really concerned about the state of your soul. Get to Jesus.

Personal Reflection: What is God saying to Me?

Matthew 5:48 AMP

You, therefore, will be perfect [growing into spiritual maturity both in mind and character, actively integrating godly values into your daily life], as your Heavenly Father is perfect.

Know this is a call to holiness and perfection. To be conformed to the image of Jesus Christ requires a pressing into the high calling of God. It takes discipline and exactitude. The devil wants you to think the moments don't matter, but they are open doors for sin to do its greatest work. No pass season for you or others.

Personal Reflection: What is God saying to Me?

Jonah 1:4 NLT

But the LORD hurled a powerful wind over the sea, causing a violent storm that threatened to break the ship apart.

Consider the hand of God. Many people place so much weight on Satan, but what we don't consider is that it happens all under God's purview. Even more importantly, difficulty and challenges may originate from God. Consider Jonah. In all situations, seek God. He has the answer.

Personal Reflection: What is God saying to Me?

Day 66

Exodus 13:21 NIV

By day, the LORD went ahead of them in a pillar of cloud to guide them on their way, and by night in a pillar of fire to give them light, so that they could travel by day or night.

Be prepared for the shifting. Never get comfortable or complacent with God. Some will act on God's initial instruction but fail to move with God. God will not waste a moment of your life. He is strategic in where He places you and with whom. Once you've exhausted it, He may shift you.

Personal Reflection: What is God saying to Me?

Day 67

Philippians 4:13 NKJV

I can do all things through Christ who strengthens me.

Being stretched. This is a stretch for your perception of yourself, not for what your capacity actually is or for God. He wants you to uncover that limitlessness that exists in you through Him. Don't just ponder it or experiment with it; bask in the possibilities of limitless potential then act on it as the Spirit leads.

Personal Reflection: What is God saying to Me?

Day 68

2 Corinthians 12:7–10 NET

Therefore, so that I would not become arrogant, a thorn in the flesh was given to me, a messenger of Satan to trouble me—so that I would not become arrogant. I asked the Lord three times about this, that it would depart from me. But He said to me, "My grace is enough for you, for my power is made perfect in weakness." So then, I will boast most gladly about my weaknesses, so that the power of Christ may reside in me. Therefore I am content with weaknesses, with insults, with troubles, with persecutions and difficulties for the sake of Christ, for whenever I am weak, then I am strong.

Let us thank God for all of the struggle and hardship. Thank you, God, for our light affliction. If it keeps us drawn to you, seeking you, dependent on you, continue. I never want to be so far outside of you that you become but a memory or a talking point. Humble me to you Lord.

Personal Reflection: What is God saying to Me?

DAY 69

Job 23:8-10 BSB

If I go east, He is not there, and if I go west, I cannot find Him. When He is at work in the north, I cannot behold Him; when He turns to the south, I cannot see Him. Yet He knows the way I have taken; when He has tested me, I will come forth as gold.

Trust God even when you can't trace Him or you. He may not only want you there but may have led you there purposely. Where? To the end of yourself, out in the deep with nothing to grasp hold of but Him. Lay hold of Jesus.

Personal Reflection: What is God saying to Me?

James 4:6 ESV

But He gives more grace. Therefore, it says, "God opposes the proud but gives grace to the humble."

God got you. He knows exactly how much rope to give you before He needs to tug on you and pull you back in. Often, what you are experiencing is a result of God shaking that rope because you went on too far. Know that you cannot get too far from God. He got you. Just go back in.

Personal Reflection: What is God saying to Me?

Matthew 10:16 CEV

So, be as wise as snakes and as innocent as doves.

For those who have given up on their lives, don't let them drain you of yours. Satan shows up as more than just one with horns or evil you can detect. He shows up in people who will slow, hinder, stop, depress, and suppress you. Don't let people steal your life. Give them over to Jesus.

Matthew 16:24 BSB

Then Jesus told His disciples, "If anyone wants to come after Me, he must deny himself and take up his cross and follow Me."

Do you want to go after Jesus and be His disciple? We must first tell ourselves the truth we know about ourselves, then submit that to Jesus so that He may reveal truth to us. If you do not want to study under, imitate, and follow the steps of the Lord, make that your prayer point.

Personal Reflection: What is God saying to Me?

Day 73

1 Kings 19:11-12 NKJV

Then He said, "Go out, and stand on the mountain before the Lord." And behold, the Lord passed by, and a great and strong wind tore into the mountains and broke the rocks in pieces before the Lord, but the Lord was not in the wind; and after the wind, an earthquake, but the Lord was not in the earthquake; and after the earthquake, a fire, but the Lord was not in the fire; and after the fire, a still small voice.

Do you know Jesus? Do you know His character, heart, will and voice? Do you want to? If so, bring that to the Lord. Seek Him with everything you have. Trust that Jesus will meet you there in the process because He wants to be known of you and wants to know you.

Personal Reflection: What is God saying to Me?

Day 74

Joel 2:12 NLT

That is why the Lord says, "Turn to me now, while there is time. Give me your hearts. Come with fasting, weeping, and mourning.

Don't give up when you err; just repent and press on. Satan wants you wrapped up in guilt, shame, and despair because it will hinder your progress, even paralyze you. Return to God, ask for forgiveness, and move forward.

Personal Reflection: What is God saying to Me?

Matthew 3:8 ESV

Bear fruit in keeping with repentance.

I repented for taking back control for a day. You see, I understand sin as not just murder, lying, or adultery, but also anything that is outside of the will of God. Yesterday, I was tired and moved outside of His will, doing what I wanted. He forgave me, and we are moving forward. It's that simple.

Personal Reflection: What is God saying to Me?

Day 76

James 4:13-15 NIV

Now listen, you who say, "Today or tomorrow we will go to this or that city, spend a year there, carry on business and make money." Why, you do not even know what will happen tomorrow. What is your life? You are a mist that appears for a little while and then vanishes. Instead, you ought to say, "If it is the Lord's will, we will live and do this or that."

What does your plan for the day or year look like? If you can say it, have you surrendered to God? We shouldn't know what the future looks like or our next moment as we live for God. It is His to dictate. Have you truly lost your life to Him? Then the future belongs to Him.

Personal Reflection: What is God saying to Me?

Romans 3:23 NKJV

For all have sinned and fall short of the glory of God.

You will triumph and fail. We all fall short of glory, and we are all kept in the humility of knowing we need a Savior.

Personal Reflection: What is God saying to Me?

Day 78

1 Kings 19:1-5 CEV

Ahab told his wife Jezebel what Elijah had done and that he had killed the prophets. She sent a message to Elijah: "You killed my prophets. Now I'm going to kill you! I pray that the gods will punish me even more severely if I don't do it by this time tomorrow."

Elijah was afraid when he got her message, and he ran to the town of Beersheba in Judah. He left his servant there, then walked another whole day into the desert. Finally, he came to a large bush and sat down in its shade. He begged the Lord, "I've had enough. Just let me die! I'm no better off than my ancestors." Then he lay down in the shade and fell asleep.

Know that this is a real lifelong walk with Jesus. You will have great moments like Elijah where you can face hundreds of false prophets with the faith in and faithfulness of your Father in Heaven, but you will also turn in the next and run in fear from mere threats of death. In those moments, ask God to help you with your unbelief.

Personal Reflection: What is God saying to Me?

DAY 79

Matthew 7:21-23 ESV

Not everyone who says to me, 'Lord, Lord,' will enter the kingdom of heaven, but the one who does the will of my Father who is in heaven. On that day many will say to me, 'Lord, Lord, did we not prophesy in your name, and cast out demons in your name, and do many mighty works in your name?' And then will I declare to them, 'I never knew you; depart from me.'

Depart from me, I don't know you. It pains me to know many are not living as Christ intends. Christians are doing God stuff without the leading and guiding of God. You can dedicate your life to God activity but never know God and be rejected when your day comes. Seek to know Jesus. Follow Him.

Personal Reflection: What is God saying to Me?

John 16:13 NIV

But when he, the Spirit of truth, comes, he will guide you into all the truth. He will not speak on his own; he will speak only what he hears, and he will tell you what is yet to come.

I experienced a spiritual attack. It was fatigue, tiredness, exhaustion, feeling like I was walking through mud carrying a heavy weight. I was unhappy, unmotivated. The Holy Spirit told me to fight, continue with my day, and make a video. I listened and felt instantly lighter. Seek the Holy Spirit for an explanation for what is occurring. He will lead you and guide you into all truth.

Personal Reflection: What is God saying to Me?

2 Timothy 2:21 ERV

The Lord wants to use you for special purposes, so make yourself clean from all evil. Then you will be holy, and the Master can use you. You will be ready for any good work.

God is ready to use many people. How much longer will you deny, resist, and rebel against God? You have done all you can in the natural. He is calling you now to shift to the spiritual realm. He is calling you so He may reveal Himself to you, make His home in you and operate through you.

Personal Reflection: What is God saying to Me?

Day 82

1 Timothy 3:4 ESV

He must manage his own household well, with all dignity, keeping his children submissive.

Warning shot from God for fathers, husbands, heads of households: God is calling you not to lead a family your way but in God's ways and thoughts. Generations and bloodlines are at stake, and He desires your full surrender so that He may use you as the covering for that family.

Personal Reflection: What is God saying to Me?

Day 83

John 4:34 NKJV

Jesus said to them, "My food is to do the will of Him who sent Me, and to finish His work."

Are you distracted? What has your full attention? Is it God and His will? Are you consumed with what God desires for you in the moment and beyond? If not, what is it—job, family, self? All should be surrendered and submitted to God. If so, there should be of no concern as you trust Him.

Personal Reflection: What is God saying to Me?

DAY 84

James 1:5 NIV

If any of you lacks wisdom, you should ask God, who gives generously to all without finding fault, and it will be given to you.

Reconsider what it is that you need. What is it that you are asking for? God desires to get you to an expected end and sets up an environment conducive to getting you there. Instead of asking Him for change, renewal, or a new thing, ask for revelation, understanding, and strategy.

Personal Reflection: What is God saying to Me?

Day 85

John 5:39-40

You study the Scriptures diligently because you think that in them you have eternal life. These are the very Scriptures that testify about me, yet you refuse to come to me to have life.

Relationship with the Word. You need scripture and you need a rhema word—a right-now word for what is occurring with you, right now in real time based on who you are, where you are, where you've been, and where God is taking you. This comes from the Holy Spirit. Get to know His voice.

Personal Reflection: What is God saying to Me?

Matthew 10:33 NIV

But whoever disowns me before others, I will disown before my Father in Heaven.

I felt out of sorts as I was surrounded by worldly people. I realized I had lost my life and myself to God. How do I be His amongst those who don't know Him? He said, "Be His." God advised me not to be ashamed but boldly be His on full display and let the chips fall where they may.

Personal Reflection: What is God saying to Me?

DAY 87

Romans 16:1-3 AMP

Now I introduce and commend to you our sister Phoebe, a deaconess (servant) of the church at Cenchrea, that you may receive her in the Lord [with love and hospitality], as God's people ought to receive one another. And that you may help her in whatever matter she may require assistance from you, for she has been a helper of many, including myself.

Greet Prisca and Aquila, my fellow workers in Christ Jesus. So, what do you expect a woman who is being called to preach, teach, or pastor to do? She knows her shepherd's voice, and a stranger she will not follow. Do you want her to run from God, rebel, and be defiant to God to appease you? Know Paul doesn't apply women being silent in the church as a universal principle in his ministry, so it is not. Women, do not run from the call of God on your life. No one stop her.

Personal Reflection: What is God saying to Me?

Day 88

Galatians 5:1 AMP

It was for this freedom that Christ set us free [completely liberating us]; therefore, keep standing firm and do not be subject again to a yoke of slavery [which you once removed].

God has me so unbothered. He has sent me on a unique journey to hide me, shield me from the opinions of others, address my fears, and instill self-worth and value in me. He had me die to the church, world, and family. He freed me to do what He called me to do and can do it for you.

Personal Reflection: What is God saying to Me?

Day 89

Romans 6:13 NIV

Do not offer any part of yourself to sin as an instrument of wickedness, but rather offer yourselves to God as those who have been brought from death to life, and offer every part of yourself to Him as an instrument of righteousness.

You can't trust your own thoughts, feelings, and emotions. The thoughts you grab hold of create strongholds that your soul defends tooth and nail. They stir up emotions that you can literally feel in your skin, and once it is in the body, it's not long before it acts on it. This is how the devil uses this to use you as an instrument of sin. Mind your thoughts. Resist the devil.

Personal Reflection: What is God saying to Me?

1 Corinthians 10:13 CJB

No temptation has seized you beyond what people normally experience, and God can be trusted not to allow you to be tempted beyond what you can bear. On the contrary, along with the temptation, He will also provide the way out, so that you will be able to endure.

God places on us more than we can bear ALL OF THE TIME. People confuse the scripture on temptation and hardship. God does not tempt and will allow a way of escape and will not let you be tempted to sin beyond what you can bear but He will place us in extreme hardship so that we will call on Him.

Personal Reflection: What is God saying to Me?

Galatians 1:10 NIV

Am I now trying to win the approval of human beings, or of God? Or am I trying to please people? If I were still trying to please people, I would not be a servant of Christ.

Not feeling somebody? This is not a personal challenge for you to try new strategies, try harder, or do more. This is the Holy Spirit letting you know the spirit in them is different and to stay away from this person. The Holy Spirit still works and is leading and guiding you.

Personal Reflection: What is God saying to Me?

Day 92

Matthew 16:23

Get behind me, Satan! You are a hindrance to me. For you are not setting your mind on the things of God, but on the things of man.

Just know and expect Satan to show up. So when tasks can't get completed, interruptions keep happening or people say something flip to you, it may catch you off guard in the moment but instead of letting it eat you alive you can just brush it off and say nice try satan and move on.

Personal Reflection: What is God saying to Me?

Day 93

Matthew 26:74 GW

Then Peter began to curse and swear with an oath, "I don't know the man!"

What is your fault? What is the one thing that, if we witness you doing, we need to start spiritually warring? See, what might be normal for others is not normal for everyone. If you see me cussing, fist-fighting, hanging on a man, drinking, or smoking, I need you to invite Jesus onto the scene now in prayer because something has got on me. If you see me twerking, grab a priest—something got in me!

Personal Reflection: What is God saying to Me?

DAY 94

Jeremiah 1:4–5 GW

The Lord spoke His word to me: "Before I formed you in the womb, I knew you. Before you were born, I set you apart for My holy purpose. I appointed you to be a prophet to the nations."

Don't limit God to your experience with God. Just because God has not done that with you does not mean God does not do that. How He moves in, through, and with another is unique to that individual and God. You may be in a different season or path.

Personal Reflection: What is God saying to Me?

DAY 95

Psalm 91:1-2 GW

Whoever lives under the shelter of the Most High will remain in the shadow of the Almighty. I will say to the Lord, "You are my refuge and my fortress, my God in whom I trust."

It has to be just you and God. There comes a time when you need to pull away from the influence of others and place your full attention on God. People, even in love, will want to spare you from God's processing. Go away with God and let Him transform you into pure gold.

Personal Reflection: What is God saying to Me?

DAY 96

Matthew 16:13-17 NIV

When Jesus came to the region of Caesarea Philippi, he asked his disciples, "Who do people say the Son of Man is?" They replied, "Some say John the Baptist; others say Elijah; and still others, Jeremiah or one of the prophets." "But what about you?" he asked. "Who do you say I am?" Simon Peter answered, "You are the Messiah, the Son of the living God." Jesus replied, "Blessed are you, Simon son of Jonah, for this was not revealed to you by flesh and blood, but by my Father in heaven."

The weight of the voice of God. Whose voice has weight in your life? Your spouse, boss, friend, mother, child? Do they have more weight than God? All voices need to be submitted and surrendered and in alignment with God or they need to be discarded.

Personal Reflection: What is God saying to Me?

Day 97

Matthew 16:26 ESV

For what will it profit a man if he gains the whole world and forfeits his soul? Or what shall a man give in return for his soul?

How to get out of the matrix? How to get out of the world's system? Go after God with everything you have. Make Him the highest priority. Let Him reveal the matrix, the world Satan created for you, and the strategy to come out of it.

Personal Reflection: What is God saying to Me?

Galatians 5:16-17 NLT

So I say, let the Holy Spirit guide your lives. Then you won't be doing what your sinful nature craves. The sinful nature wants to do evil, which is just the opposite of what the Spirit wants. And the Spirit gives us desires that are the opposite of what the sinful nature desires. These two forces are constantly fighting each other, so you are not free to carry out your good intentions.

Feed your spirit man. Are you feeding or starving your spirit man? How full is your flesh with its lust, ego, and vanities? Which is leading in your life? Evaluate, then adjust your daily activities to so you weaken the enemy of God (flesh) and strengthen your spirit man.

Personal Reflection: What is God saying to Me?

Day 99

Isaiah 43:21 ESV

The people whom I formed for myself, that they might declare my praise.

What is innate is meant for God. It is built into us as God has formed us to worship, seek, follow, and surrender. Know that if you do not direct these inclinations to God, Satan will steal them and redirect them to the world, of which he is the ruler of.

Personal Reflection: What is God saying to Me?

Galatians 6:9 ESV

And let us not grow weary of doing good, for in due season we will reap if we do not give up.

I spoke to God and told Him that as I follow Him, I'm bored, tired, and exhausted. He explained this is exactly where He wants me, as this is when I give up. I needed to learn how to stay committed and work through these negative feelings.

Personal Reflection: What is God saying to Me?

Day 101

1 Peter 5:7 AMP

Casting all your cares [all your anxieties, all your worries, and all your concerns, once and for all] on Him, for He cares about you [with deepest affection and watches over you very carefully].

I am lucky to have God. I was going through such difficulty, and as I brought my concerns to Him, He brought me clarity, understanding, and strategy. He, as a loving Father, helped me see my way through. I now feel hopeful and lighter. You have access to the same God. Try Him.

Personal Reflection: What is God saying to Me?

DAY 102

Ephesians 6:11-12 NLT

Put on all of God's armor so that you will be able to stand firm against all strategies of the devil. For we are not fighting against flesh-and-blood enemies, but against evil rulers and authorities of the unseen world, against mighty powers in this dark world, and against evil spirits in the heavenly places.

What is going on in the spiritual realm? Know that God and Satan are at work. Armed with this knowledge, the only choice you have is to partner with God. He needs to walk you into destiny, all while giving you all that is required for you to defeat the wiles and schemes of Satan.

Personal Reflection: What is God saying to Me?

DAY 103

John 8:44 NIV

You belong to your father, the devil, and you want to carry out your father's desires. He was a murderer from the beginning, not holding to the truth, for there is no truth in him. When he lies, he speaks his native language, for he is a liar and the father of lies.

Get free from Satan. The father of lies is lying to you. How? He is killing, stealing, destroying, and devouring in your life. How? Can you admit this? What is your strategy for it? Is it working? Surrender and partner with God. He is the only one who can defeat Satan.

Personal Reflection: What is God saying to Me?

Luke 10:19 ESV

Behold, I have given you authority to tread on serpents and scorpions, and over all the power of the enemy, and nothing shall hurt you.

You better not stand in fear of Satan. If it's your day to come face to face with Satan be sure to meet him there with Jesus. You already stand in victory with Jesus. We don't threaten or call out Satan, but we do stand in our authority fearlessly in the name of Jesus.

Personal Reflection: What is God saying to Me?

Day 105

Exodus 9:16 NKJV

But indeed for this purpose I have raised you up, that I may show My power in you, and that My name may be declared in all the earth.

"God in me. Destiny and Me. We are one in three." This is a phrase the Lord gave me. God wants to take you into destiny. You can't get to your final destination without God. You must commit to God and destiny and accept that you are one in three.

2 Corinthians 3:18 NIV

And we all, who with unveiled faces contemplate the Lord's glory, are being transformed into His image with ever-increasing glory, which comes from the Lord, who is the Spirit.

I am in awe of what God has done in my life. He has transformed me and my life. I used to try to be bold and courageous. I would try to believe in myself and have self-worth. I would try so hard. It was all a show, an effort. After time with God, I am.

Personal Reflection: What is God saying to Me?

Isaiah 55:11 NIV

So is my word that goes out from my mouth: it will not return to me empty, but will accomplish what I desire and achieve the purpose for which I sent it.

What is God doing in your life? Do you know? See, God spoke a word over you when you were born, and God's word does not go out and return void. He also watches over it to make sure it's fulfilled. He is more active in your life than you know. Ask Him for understanding. Surrender.

Personal Reflection: What is God saying to Me?

Matthew 16:25 DLNT

For whoever wants to save his life will lose it. But whoever loses his life for My sake will find it.

God asks, "When will you get serious about me? When will you deny yourself comfort, control, the need to know? When will you go into the depths of Me? Will you go to the edge but jump off the cliff? What I need to extract from you cannot happen in comfort. It happens during flight."

Personal Reflection: What is God saying to Me?

1 Timothy 6:9 NLT

Yet true godliness with contentment is itself great wealth. After all, we brought nothing with us when we came into the world, and we can't take anything with us when we leave it. So, if we have enough food and clothing, let us be content.

But people who long to be rich fall into temptation and are trapped by many foolish and harmful desires that plunge them into ruin and destruction.

I asked God, "Why am I leaning into suffering?" He said it's because I have learned to kill the need but also that suffering was an illusion I was no longer under. I had nothing and was fine. Suffering is due to perceived lack of need. If you died to Christ, then know, dead men don't have needs. And Satan cannot kill a dead man.

Personal Reflection: What is God saying to Me?

Acts 10:9-15 NIV

About noon the following day, as they were on their journey and approaching the city, Peter went up on the roof to pray. He became hungry and wanted something to eat, and while the meal was being prepared, he fell into a trance. He saw heaven opened and something like a large sheet being let down to earth by its four corners. It contained all kinds of four-footed animals, as well as reptiles and birds. Then a voice told him, "Get up, Peter. Kill and eat." "Surely not, Lord!" Peter replied. "I have never eaten anything impure or unclean." The voice spoke to him a second time, "Do not call anything impure that God has made clean."

Peter did not want to eat the animals because the law prevented him. God used this to show him He wanted Peter to visit a Gentile house, which was also unlawful. Peter obeyed and witnessed to them. As a result, the Holy Spirit came on all who heard the message; they were speaking in tongues, praising God, and baptized in the name of Jesus Christ. Be open to the new thing God is doing.

Personal Reflection: What is God saying to Me?

Mark 2:24; 27-28 NLT

But the Pharisees said to Jesus, "Look, why are they breaking the law by harvesting grain on the Sabbath?"

Then Jesus said to them, "The Sabbath was made to meet the needs of people, and not people to meet the requirements of the Sabbath. So the Son of Man is Lord, even over the Sabbath!"

Should women preach, among other things? Do what God is telling you to do. People quoted Scripture to Jesus all the time, trying to challenge and trap Him. Jesus was trying to move them beyond the law to its fulfillment. Don't let people trap you in Scripture if they don't understand it. Women being silent in church is not a universal principle, and Paul doesn't apply it as such across His ministry. Do what God says.

Personal Reflection: What is God saying to Me?

Day 112

Romans 10:9-10 GW

If you declare that Jesus is Lord...

Is Jesus Lord over your life? Can He at any given moment shift you? Can He tell you today is your last day on the job, in a relationship or living in a location? Can He change your identity? Can He change your day, moment? If not, is He really your Lord or are you?

Personal Reflection: What is God saying to Me?

Jeremiah 29:12-13 NLV

"Then you will call upon Me and come and pray to Me, and I will listen to you. You will look for Me and find Me, when you look for Me with all your heart. I will be found by you," says the Lord.

God desires for us to seek and follow His voice. He does not want us in routine, control, in the know, stuck in fixed points, imprisoned by our own ideas and ways. He wants us free and available to serve and obey Him at any given moment.

Personal Reflection: What is God saying to Me?

Psalm 63:1-4 ESV

O God, you are my God; earnestly I seek you; my soul thirsts for you; my flesh faints for you, as in a dry and weary land where there is no water. So I have looked upon you in the sanctuary, beholding your power and glory. Because your steadfast love is better than life, my lips will praise you. So I will bless you as long as I live; in your name I will lift up my hands.

Yes, you should read Scripture. You need the information for a solid foundation. It is God Himself and the written aspect of Him you should know. But understand you should seek a relationship with the Word. What is He asking you to do today, right now at this moment?

Personal Reflection: What is God saying to Me?

DAY 115

Galatians 2:19-21 MSG

What actually took place is this: I tried keeping rules and working my head off to please God, and it didn't work. So I quit being a "law man" so that I could be God's man. Christ's life showed me how, and enabled me to do it. I identified myself completely with him. Indeed, I have been crucified with Christ. My ego is no longer central. It is no longer important that I appear righteous before you or have your good opinion, and I am no longer driven to impress God. Christ lives in me. The life you see me living is not "mine," but it is lived by faith in the Son of God, who loved me and gave himself for me. I am not going to go back on that.

I tried to be a posterchild, Christian. I used to try to act good. I would try to be perfect. I tried to be nice, kind and loving. Now I know that I am God's. I embrace that I am His. I merely now instead of acting or trying, I obey God.

Personal Reflection: What is God saying to Me?

Day 116

Jeremiah 29:11 NLV

For I know the plans I have for you,' says the Lord, 'plans for well-being and not for trouble, to give you a future and a hope.

Did you know you are not supposed to be figuring out the plan because God has one to prosper you? The steps of a righteous man are ordered. Take the step, and the next one will be revealed. How? Go after God, deny yourself, take up your cross, follow Him. Make time for Him. Seek Him diligently. Surrender and obey.

Personal Reflection: What is God saying to Me?

James 2:26 ESV

For as the body apart from the spirit is dead, so also faith apart from works is dead.

Balancing faith and works. I asked God, "How do I balance this faith, rest with works?" He told me that it is a strategy of the devil to confuse people and make them think there is a formula or that they are doing something wrong. He said, "Get up, take up your cross and follow me.

Personal Reflection: What is God saying to Me?

2 Corinthians 12:9 NIV

But he said to me, "My grace is sufficient for you, for my power is made perfect in weakness."

In this walk, I have not been perfect. I have walked away from God. I have run. I have even been brought so low I considered Satan, even suicide. I am not perfect. I am God's. In all my doing—good, bad, and ugly—it all served a purpose, and I am still His all because of His grace.

Personal Reflection: What is God saying to Me?

John 14:23 NKJV

Jesus answered and said to him, "If anyone loves Me, he will keep My word; and My Father will love him, and We will come to him and make Our home with him.

I asked God, "How do I not overwhelm people with you? He said, "Because you have sacrificed your body to Me and I have made My home in you, I abide in you and you in Me. It is not just you that pours out; it is ME with fury, passion, boldness. Do not try to contain or suppress Me."

Personal Reflection: What is God saying to Me?

Psalm 37:23 NLT

The Lord directs the steps of the godly. He delights in every detail of their lives.

My life with God may seem strange to you. He guides my every step. I wake and go to bed to Him. He is in charge of every aspect of my day. It took years to build up to this point with much coming and going. But here we are, completely surrendered, completely His (most days).

Personal Reflection: What is God saying to Me?

Luke 14:26 NLT

If you want to be my disciple, you must, by comparison, hate everyone else—your father and mother, wife and children, brothers and sisters—yes, even your own life. Otherwise, you cannot be my disciple.

Placing people under God and not as God. I will no longer give people the right to make me feel fearful, small, or less than. Many I don't ask for opinions and don't care for. Many hold no major role in my life. Today, I take my power back. All I need is God. Devil, access denied.

Personal Reflection: What is God saying to Me?

Matthew 6:33 ESV

But seek first the kingdom of God and His righteousness, and all these things will be added to you.

Have you given your soul over to Satan? Who has your whole soul—your mind, will, and emotions? Is it bent toward this world? Is it bent toward yourself? Satan is the ruler of this world, worships himself, and desires you to worship Him. If Jesus doesn't have your whole soul, who does?

Personal Reflection: What is God saying to Me?

Day 123

2 Corinthians 4:4 ERV

The ruler of this world has blinded the minds of those who don't believe. They cannot see the light of the Good News—the message about the divine greatness of Christ. Christ is the one who is exactly like God.

See, at least people that sell their soul to Satan have done so and received a return. Have you, as in Ezekiel 16, given your soul away to the enemy and this world of his for free? If Jesus doesn't have your soul, then the world does. The ruler of this world is Satan, so he has your soul.

Personal Reflection: What is God saying to Me?

Luke 12:34 ESV

For where your treasure is, there will your heart be also.

What would it take for you to sell yourself over to Satan? Ezekiel 16 calls the people of Israel prostitutes because they go after other gods. In God's eyes, they are adulterous. The Lord is our husband, as Isaiah 54 states. Are you going after other gods?

Personal Reflection: What is God saying to Me?

Day 125: Christmas

Luke 2:11-14 NKJV

For there is born to you this day in the city of David a Savior, who is Christ the Lord. And this will be the sign to you: You will find a Babe wrapped in swaddling cloths, lying in a manger. And suddenly there was with the angel a multitude of the heavenly host praising God and saying, "Glory to God in the highest, And on earth peace, goodwill toward men!"

Satan wants to take Christ of Christmas, and for many he has as they celebrate XMAS. Reduce the focus on things outside of Christ and find one activity you can do this year to honor the birth of Christ.

Personal Reflection: What is God saying to Me?

1 Peter 2:11 DARBY

Beloved, I exhort [you], as strangers and sojourners, to abstain from fleshly lusts, which war against the soul;

Be sure to place Christ first in your Christmas. The world has informed us on how to celebrate Christmas. It's all money, greed, consumerism, self, tireless activity, burnout, self-aggrandizement, but nothing of Christ. Satan wants to take Christ of Christmas. Don't let him this year.

Personal Reflection: What is God saying to Me?

Genesis 24:12-14 NIRV

Then he prayed, "Lord, you are the God of my master Abraham. Make me successful today. Be kind to my master Abraham. I'm standing beside this spring. The daughters of the people who live in the town are coming out here to get water. I will speak to a young woman. I'll say to her, 'Please lower your jar so I can have a drink.' Suppose she says, 'Have a drink of water, and I'll get some for your camels too.' Then let her be the one you have chosen for your servant Isaac. That's how I'll know you have been kind to my master."

Abraham sent his servant away to find his son a wife. His servant seeks God for guidance. Let God choose your mate. God's wisdom and timing is perfect. In your singleness or divine separation from your spouse, He is building, molding, shaping, restoring, healing, training, and preparing them and you. You do not want to cut that process short. Trust God.

Personal Reflection: What is God saying to Me?

Genesis 17-27 ESV

"Should I hide my plan from Abraham?" the Lord asked. So the Lord told Abraham, "I have heard a great outcry from Sodom and Gomorrah, because their sin is so flagrant. I am going down to see if their actions are as wicked as I have heard. If not, I want to know." The other men turned and headed toward Sodom, but the Lord remained with Abraham. Abraham approached him and said, "Will you sweep away both the righteous and the wicked?" "Suppose you find fifty righteous people living there in the city—will you still sweep it away and not spare it for their sakes? Surely you wouldn't do such a thing, destroying the righteous along with the wicked. Why, you would be treating the righteous and the wicked exactly the same! Surely you wouldn't do that! Should not the Judge of all the earth do what is right?" And the Lord replied, "If I find fifty righteous people in Sodom, I will spare the entire city for their sake." Then Abraham spoke again.

What I didn't know about God is that He actually talks to you conversationally. I didn't know that His Spirit was literally inside of me and can be accessed at any moment and would really lead and guide my every move. I didn't know I would have a relationship with Jesus. You can too. If you do, you can always go deeper in Him.

Personal Reflection: What is God saying to Me?

2 Peter 3:18 ESV

But grow in the grace and knowledge of our Lord and Savior Jesus Christ. To Him be the glory both now and to the day of eternity. Amen.

Has your spirituality changed over the years? God is expansive, inexhaustible, eternal. Question if you are leaning into God because, if so, you should be growing and having new experiences often, if not daily.

Personal Reflection: What is God saying to Me?

Ephesians 6:13 NKJV

Therefore, take up the whole armor of God, that you may be able to withstand in the evil day, and having done all, to stand.

What is your beef with God? You have died to Christ. You have been crucified with Him. You have denied yourself. You have given your body as a living sacrifice to Him right? So, what is your complaint? Does it start with I? Who are you? You are God's. Pay attention to the shift. Is there a shift in how you feel? Do you suddenly feel weighed down, heavy, tired, sad, bored, etc.? This is the work of Satan. He wants you to feel hopeless and to give up on life itself and walk away from God. Stand! Spiritually, go to war. Stand.

Personal Reflection: What is God saying to Me?

Ephesians 4:27 ESV

And give no opportunity to the Devil.

Know Satan's strategy. Satan wants you dead. He wants you to sell him your soul. He wants you to publicly renounce God. He wants you apart from God and doubting or even hating Him. He wants to kill, steal, destroy, and devour in your life by your very own hand.

Personal Reflection: What is God saying to Me?

1 Peter 5:8 ESV

Be sober-minded; be watchful. Your adversary, the devil, prowls around like a roaring lion, seeking someone to devour.

Satan is always at work. Be sober. Be vigilant. Your adversary is looking for opportunities to keep you small, hurt, neglected, and rejected. He wants to keep you out of your true identity in Christ and away from God. He is always working through people and your thoughts.

Personal Reflection: What is God saying to Me?

John 15:4 NKJV

Abide in Me, and I in you. As the branch cannot bear fruit of itself, unless it abides in the vine, neither can you, unless you abide in Me.

It's not about you or me. I am no different from you. The same power that works in healers, prophets, demonic deliverers, apostles, preachers, teachers, evangelists, etc., is the same power available to you to express itself uniquely in you. The Spirit of God is available for all to abide in and for Him to abide in you.

Personal Reflection: What is God saying to Me?

1 Corinthians 6:19-20 NIV

Do you not know that your bodies are temples of the Holy Spirit, who is in you, whom you have received from God? You are not your own; you were bought at a price. Therefore honor God with your bodies.

You are not your own. However God decides to use you is His prerogative. When you give your body over as a living sacrifice to God you die to yourself. You deny yourself. You take up your cross and follow Him wherever He leads you. Dead men don't feel. So, what is your complaint?

Personal Reflection: What is God saying to Me?

Proverbs 18:21 KJV

Death and life are in the power of the tongue, and they that love it shall eat the fruit thereof.

Know the authority you have in Jesus Christ and stand on it. You have the power of death and life on your tongue. You can prophesy to dry bones in your life. Jesus is the resurrection. There is power through Him. Stop lying down and getting beaten up by the devil. Fight back.

Personal Reflection: What is God saying to Me?

Ephesians 6:12 NIV

For our struggle is not against flesh and blood, but against the rulers, against the authorities, against the powers of this dark world, and against the spiritual forces of evil in the heavenly realms.

Spiritually war Ephesians six. Pray against rulers, authorities, powers of this dark world & the spiritual forces of evil in the heavenly realms working in every arena, relationship & aspect of your being. Denounce, Bind, Decree, Cast out, Release, Command, Cover, Manifest, Activate, Speak the word.

Personal Reflection: What is God saying to Me?

DAY 137

Romans 12:3 NRSVA

For by the grace given to me, I say to everyone among you not to think of yourself more highly than you ought to think, but to think with sober judgement, each according to the measure of faith that God has assigned.

Deal with your Messiah complex. You cannot and are not supposed to save everyone. This is the job of Jesus. Be sure to create a healthy distance as you care for and have compassion for others. People need to have room on their spiritual walks for the highs and lows to bring to Jesus.

Personal Reflection: What is God saying to Me?

Isaiah 65:24 NIV

Before they call I will answer; while they are yet speaking I will hear.

What if God is not responding? He may not be responding in the way that you desire but make no mistake, He has heard your prayers. He knows what it is you are experiencing. He knows what you stand in need of. The perceived silence has purpose. Rest assured God is at work.

Personal Reflection: What is God saying to Me?

1 John 1:9 NIV

If we confess our sins, he is faithful and just and will forgive us our sins and purify us from all unrighteousness

It's never too late to return to God. No matter what you have done; no matter how long it has been; no matter the need, go to God. He's waiting with open arms to receive you. God is not a human with fickle emotions. As your heavenly Father, He simply desires your return.

Personal Reflection: What is God saying to Me?

Day 140

2 Corinthians 13:5 ESV

Examine yourselves, to see whether you are in the faith. Test yourselves. Or do you not realize this about yourselves, that Jesus Christ is in you?—unless indeed you fail to meet the test!

James 4:7 ESV

Submit yourselves therefore to God.

Tell yourself the truth. Bring that before the Lord. Ask Him to help you navigate that and give you strategy on how to deal with it.

Personal Reflection: What is God saying to Me?

DAY 141

2 Corinthians 9:8 ESV

And God is able to make all grace abound to you, so that having all sufficiency in all things at all times, you may abound in every good work.

What is God asking you to do? Be in God's flow. His grace, favor is on the time when He asks you to do something. Do not hesitate, question simply move with God.

Personal Reflection: What is God saying to Me?

2 Timothy 2:21 ERV

The Lord wants to use you for special purposes, so make yourself clean from all evil. Then you will be holy, and the Master can use you. You will be ready for any good work.

God needs you. Don't ever think that you are expendable or not of value to God. God created you with intentionality, purpose. You were made as a response to a need in this world. The harvest is much but the laborers are few. God not only wants you but needs you.

Personal Reflection: What is God saying to Me?

John 4:34 NIV

"My food," said Jesus, "is to do the will of him who sent me and to finish his work."

Are God's desires your desires? Do your actions show that you care for what God wants? Do you seek Him early? Do you involve Him in your daily decisions? What drives you in your daily activity? Is it God?

Personal Reflection: What is God saying to Me?

Proverbs 14:12 ESV

There is a way that seems right to a man, but its end is the way to death.

What makes life hard is your resistance, your need to control, and to know. Take your hands off of situations and let them breathe. Give God a chance to move in and breathe on those situations. Give people room to step up.

Personal Reflection: What is God saying to Me?

Day 145

Philippians 4:6 ESV

Do not be anxious about anything, but in everything by prayer and supplication with thanksgiving let your requests be made known to God.

What are you afraid of? Admit your fears, face them, and bring them before the Lord. Where is your faith and trust in God? If you show up as your true self in Christ and do the best that you can, that is enough. He will take care of the rest.

Personal Reflection: What is God saying to Me?

Psalm 147:3 ESV

He heals the brokenhearted and binds up their wounds.

The best thing you can do for anyone or anything is to heal. Healing will not only change you and others around you, it will change your environments. There will be a shift as you show up differently. The world must respond accordingly.

Personal Reflection: What is God saying to Me?

Day 147

2 Corinthians 5:17 ESV

Therefore, if anyone is in Christ, he is a new creation. The old has passed away; behold, the new has come.

Never give up hope. It is never hopeless. Some things must die in order for them to have new life. Is this not the power of the gospel message, resurrection? Prophesy to the dry bones in your life; use the power of the tongue to speak life into your situations. Don't give up.

Personal Reflection: What is God saying to Me?

Romans 8:28 ESV

And we know that for those who love God all things work together for good, for those who are called according to his purpose.

I asked God, "Why does suffering happen?" His response was that I will never understand as I view it through a limited human lens. Christ was crucified. It was God who was present in and suffered with Him. It is He who is with us and suffers with us. The rest remains, as He is, a mystery.

Personal Reflection: What is God saying to Me?

Ephesians 4:22–24 ESV

To put off your old self, which belongs to your former manner of life and is corrupt through deceitful desires, and to be renewed in the spirit of your minds, and to put on the new self, created after the likeness of God in true righteousness and holiness.

Are you getting tired, burnt out on life? Are people, things, and activities losing their interest? Understand that God desires to bring you into new life, but He must burn off the desire for the old to bring you into the new, transitioning you from the world's system to kingdom living.

Personal Reflection: What is God saying to Me?

Ephesians 5:22-24 NIV

Wives, submit yourselves to your own husbands as you do to the Lord. For the husband is the head of the wife, as Christ is the head of the church, His body, of which he is the Savior. Now as the church submits to Christ, so also wives should submit to their husbands in everything.

Submission in marriage is God's will for the wife. This is the proper order of the household. As a woman, when you are out of the order and authority of the family established by God, you open yourself up and give you and therefore your household access to the enemy to wreak havoc. Stay in order, stay in position.

Personal Reflection: What is God saying to Me?

Proverbs 13:20 ESV

Whoever walks with the wise becomes wise, but the companion of fools will suffer harm.

Who is it that you need to untangle yourself from? Who is it that you feel uncomfortable with? Who is it that, despite your best efforts, continues to use you or is mean and dismissive of you? Create distance or even let go. They are not for you. Love yourself enough to put you first.

Personal Reflection: What is God saying to Me?

Proverbs 4:23 NLT

Guard your heart above all else, for it determines the course of your life.

Why couldn't I love? God explained to me that He had hardened my heart so I could not. It was time for me to protect and safeguard myself and put myself first. I couldn't love, despite my efforts, because it was time for me to let them go.

Personal Reflection: What is God saying to Me?

Day 153

3 John 1:2 ESV

Beloved, I pray that all may go well with you and that you may be in good health, as it goes well with your soul.

God is for you. When you come to know how much God loves you and desires for you to be healed, loved, and living in authenticity, you begin to trust Him. You may not understand and even be resistant to what He is doing in the moment, but You will know that it is for your ultimate good.

Personal Reflection: What is God saying to Me?

Isaiah 55:8-9 NKJV

"For My thoughts are not your thoughts, Nor are your ways My ways," says the Lord.

"For as the heavens are higher than the earth, So are My ways higher than your ways, And My thoughts than your thoughts."

Mom story. God released me from the care and responsibility of my mom. I never knew her growing up but came to start as an older adult. She didn't want to help herself, and God told me I was no longer to help her either. Our job is not to do what we think the right thing to do is but what God says. He knows best.

Personal Reflection: What is God saying to Me?

James 2:19 ESV

You believe that God is one; you do well. Even the demons believe—and shudder!

When are you going to fight? Stop giving yourself passes! Stop playing with God. Your very soul is at stake. This is serious. This is not just about you but about everything and everyone attached to you! Get in the fight, get free!

Personal Reflection: What is God saying to Me?

Day 156

1 Samuel 16:7 ESV

But the Lord said to Samuel, "Do not look on his appearance or on the height of his stature, because I have rejected him. For the Lord sees not as man sees: man looks on the outward appearance, but the Lord looks on the heart."

God desires your heart. He wants you—not your perfection, your false character, your performance—but you. You don't have to figure it out. He already has. He just wants your heart. He will take care of the rest. Go to Him. It's time. He's waiting.

Personal Reflection: What is God saying to Me?

Day 157

Isaiah 53:10 ESV

Yet it was the will of the Lord to crush him; He has put him to grief. When his soul makes an offering for guilt, he shall see his offspring; he shall prolong his days; the will of the Lord shall prosper in his hand.

God will crush you. People think God will never have you experience difficulty. This is not biblical. He sent Jesus to the cross, and on the other side was glory. On the other side of your crushing is God's glory revealed in and through you.

Personal Reflection: What is God saying to Me?

Psalm 28:1-2 NLT

I pray to you, O Lord, my rock. Do not turn a deaf ear to me. For if you are silent, I might as well give up and die. Listen to my prayer for mercy as I cry out to you for help, as I lift my hands toward your holy sanctuary.

The Book of Psalm is so encouraging. David and many others allow you to have a sense of community in your walk with God. They bring their whole selves to the Lord without formula or methodology. Hurt, sad, confused? Read Psalm and know you are not alone.

Personal Reflection: What is God saying to Me?

2 Corinthians 2:11 ESV

So that we would not be outwitted by Satan, for we are not ignorant of his designs.

The secret the devil does not want you to know is that he created a world system to keep you small, rejected, neglected, angry at God, self-absorbed, distracted, apart from God, from finding your true identity, and living in purpose, and is using your thoughts and people to do it.

Personal Reflection: What is God saying to Me?

2 Corinthians 4:4 ESV

In their case, the god of this world has blinded the minds of the unbelievers to keep them from seeing the light of the gospel of the glory of Christ, who is the image of God.

God told me, "People want to live apart from Me because they don't know any better. They don't know they are not supposed to do it alone but with Me or they see Me as a threat to their way of life, to who they are. They built their lives on falsehood, and I want to give them truth."

Personal Reflection: What is God saying to Me?

Matthew 6:9 NIV

Our Father in heaven, hallowed be Your name. Your kingdom come, your will be done, on earth as it is in heaven.

God uses words. He is conversational and wants to speak to you and with you. He is a real Father, and Jesus a real brother and friend. He has a specific destination for you and a unique identity with purpose that requires you not to guess but to move with clarity and certainty with God.

Personal Reflection: What is God saying to Me?

Ecclesiastes 1:14 NIV

I have seen all the things that are done under the sun; all of them are meaningless, a chasing after the wind.

Everything has been done under the sun. Don't get caught up in tasking, purpose, or assignment. Be sure to make who you are, family, and home a priority. This is where you find joy. Even in the new, as you step into purpose, it will become routine. Practice contentment where you are.

Personal Reflection: What is God saying to Me?

Isaiah 29:13 KJV

Wherefore the Lord said, "For as this people draw near me with their mouth, and with their lips do honour me, but have removed their heart far from me, and their fear toward me is taught by the precept of men."

We come to Christ acting out what we thought, as heathens, a Christian should be, how they should behave or others' opinions of Christians. We need to surrender to and seek Christ to find our identities in Him and then walk with Him as we live that out with confidence.

Personal Reflection: What is God saying to Me?

Day 164

John 1:1

In the beginning was the Word, and the Word was with God, and the Word was God.

Step beyond scripture is actually having a relationship with the Word; having a relationship with God. God wants you to do something with His word. Many people challenged Jesus with scripture, but He had to get them to understand proper application in each circumstance in real time.

Personal Reflection: What is God saying to Me?

Romans 8:38-39 NLT

And I am convinced that nothing can ever separate us from God's love. Neither death nor life, neither angels nor demons, neither our fears for today nor our worries about tomorrow—not even the powers of hell can separate us from God's love. No power in the sky above or in the earth below—indeed, nothing in all creation will ever be able to separate us from the love of God that is revealed in Christ Jesus our Lord.

My fear was that I would lose Jesus. I feared missing a step, getting off track, or becoming comfortable. God showed me how this created fear and anxiety that comes from the enemy. He reassured me that nothing could separate me from His love.

Personal Reflection: What is God saying to Me?

1 Peter 5:7 ESV

Casting all your anxieties on Him, because He cares for you.

Embrace the love of Jesus. He loves you so much and has all of your tears and prayers. Don't suppress and live with hurt, pain, and hardship. It is doing a dark work in you unaware. Instead, bring it all to Jesus, let Him pour out His love on you and bask in it.

Personal Reflection: What is God saying to Me?

John 14:6 ESV

Jesus said to him, "I am the way, and the truth, and the life. No one comes to the Father except through me."

I asked God why many don't seek Him. He responded, "Fear. Many are wrapped up in insecurities about themselves that spill over into their roles, relationships, and life, and they don't have time for Me. They are trying to secure life, not realizing I am the way, the truth, and the life."

Personal Reflection: What is God saying to Me?

Psalm 46:10 NIV

He says, "Be still, and know that I am God; I will be exalted among the nations, I will be exalted in the earth."

Be ok with being still. Many are work-aholics, go-getters, 'get 'er done folks but there is a time in which God will call you to rest. Know there is season for all and if God is telling you to rest, you may have done all He requires for Him to now do the heavy lifting. Trust Him.

Personal Reflection: What is God saying to Me?

Day 169

Genesis 2:2-3 NKJV

And on the seventh day God ended His work which He had done, and He rested on the seventh day from all His work which He had done. Then God blessed the seventh day and sanctified it, because in it He rested from all His work which God had created and made.

You deserve rest. Is your self-worth tied to your productivity? Does your completed checklist validate your worthiness of titles or lend credibility to your roles? Know there are rhythms of work and rest that even God followed. Rest or at least slow down. Deal with what comes up.

Personal Reflection: What is God saying to Me?

John 12:25 ESV

Whoever loves his life loses it, and whoever hates his life in this world will keep it for eternal life.

Pay the cost. The anointing costs. It's expensive. It is paid for with your life. You must lose your life, offer your body as a living sacrifice, take up your cross, and follow God. You cannot read, study, or practice it. It's God's doing and requires your faith and surrender.

Personal Reflection: What is God saying to Me?

Philippians 4:11-13 ESV

Not that I am speaking of being in need, for I have learned in whatever situation I am to be content. I know how to be brought low, and I know how to abound. In any and every circumstance, I have learned the secret of facing plenty and hunger, abundance and need. I can do all things through Him who strengthens me.

How to manage the duality of contentment for today and expectancy for tomorrow: The danger is not in contentment but in comfort, laziness, and stagnation of the moment. In contentment, we are satisfied and at rest in God trusting Him while moving in faith and expectancy for the next.

Personal Reflection: What is God saying to Me?

Proverbs 6:6-8 NLT

Take a lesson from the ants, you lazybones. Learn from their ways and become wise! Though they have no prince or governor or ruler to make them work, they labor hard all summer, gathering food for the winter.

Not in purpose or in your passion job? Know that we all do not have the luxury of sitting on the mountain top with God for seasons of our lives 24/7. Seek God. Trust that at any job you are developing skills and character building that will be needed for your purpose.

Personal Reflection: What is God saying to Me?

Galatians 5:26 ESV

Let us not become conceited, provoking one another, envying one another.

Don't be envious of other people's spiritual walk. God often-times exposes you to people of a different spiritual maturity to show you the possibility. You cannot force the hand of God to reveal Himself to you or engage you in a certain way. Seek God diligently and trust Him.

Personal Reflection: What is God saying to Me?

Philippians 2:8 GNV

He humbled himself, and became obedient unto the death, even the death of the cross.

Are you following in the pattern of Christ, seeking the will of the Father, then performing it? Are you showing up as a faithful ambassador of Christ? Who is leading, guiding, and governing your life?

Personal Reflection: What is God saying to Me?

John 5:19-20 NIV

Jesus gave them this answer: "Very truly I tell you, the Son can do nothing by himself; he can do only what he sees his Father doing, because whatever the Father does the Son also does. For the Father loves the Son and shows him all he does. Yes, and he will show him even greater works than these, so that you will be amazed."

Do you have the mindset of Christ, where you are about your Father's business? Do you show up in your Father's name doing what you see your Father doing? Jesus got up early to be with the Father. Do you? If not, ask Jesus to help you.

Personal Reflection: What is God saying to Me?

DAY 176

Ezekiel 16: 4;9;14;17 NIV

On the day you were born your cord was not cut, nor were you washed with water to make you clean, nor were you rubbed with salt or wrapped in cloths.

"I bathed you with water and washed the blood from you and put ointments on you.

And your fame spread among the nations on account of your beauty, because the splendor I had given you made your beauty perfect," declares the Sovereign Lord.

You also took the fine jewelry I gave you, the jewelry made of my gold and silver, and you made for yourself male idols and engaged in prostitution with them.

Are you the one God cared for, raised, and cleaned up, but yet you turned on Him? Are you the adulterous love He speaks of? Are you giving more attention to your idols than God? He does not take this lightly, and there will be consequences.

Personal Reflection: What is God saying to Me?

Day 177

Isaiah 40:29 ESV

He gives power to the faint, and to him who has no might, He increases strength.

I prayed to God when I ran out of faith on my wilderness journey; I had nothing left. But God showed me that this is when He shows up the strongest. I made it through that day and many more to come. Faith does not have to be perfect. He only needs a morsel, and my prayer was enough.

Personal Reflection: What is God saying to Me?

Matthew 18:12–14 ESV

What do you think? If a man has a hundred sheep, and one of them has gone astray, does he not leave the ninety-nine on the mountains and go in search of the one that went astray? And if he finds it, truly, I say to you, he rejoices over it more than over the ninety-nine that never went astray. So it is not the will of my Father who is in heaven that one of these little ones should perish.

Honest feelings during a wilderness journey. There were times I regretted taking up my cross and following God. There were times I questioned His love and was angry at myself for loving and obeying Him. It got hard. At times, I turned away. It was only ever temporary. God can handle your real emotions.

Personal Reflection: What is God saying to Me?

Day 179

Revelation 3:15-16 ESV

I know your works: you are neither cold nor hot. Would that you were either cold or hot! So, because you are lukewarm, and neither hot nor cold, I will spit you out of my mouth.

Get in the boat or stay out. Stop coming out of the boat when called and going back in when it gets rough. Hot or cold is one thing, but the lukewarm stuff is what Jesus cannot stand. Make a decision to get out of the boat for good and even send the boat away. Learn to walk on water.

Personal Reflection: What is God saying to Me?

John 11:42-43 BSB

I knew that You always hear Me, but I say this for the benefit of the people standing here, so they may believe that You sent Me." After Jesus had said this, He called out in a loud voice, "Lazarus, come out!"

It is so they will believe. Have you done everything you can to get results- pray, read scripture, worship, show gratitude, fast, quote God's word to Him and still nothing. It could be because He desires the situation to get dire so they may witness the come up and believe.

Personal Reflection: What is God saying to Me?

Matthew 11:28-30 NIV

"Come to me, all you who are weary and burdened, and I will give you rest. Take my yoke upon you and learn from me, for I am gentle and humble in heart, and you will find rest for your souls. For my yoke is easy and my burden is light."

Are you resting in God? Is His yoke easy and His burden light? When you trust someone has it, you rest. Do you trust God with your life, soul, and family? He's got you. Simply know He is for you and always working on your behalf, and let Him show up strong in your life.

Personal Reflection: What is God saying to Me?

James 4:8 ESV

Draw near to God, and he will draw near to you.

Let God in your devotion time. You can start with the checklist, but open it up to God and allow Him to expand it. Linger with Him, spend more time with Him, go deeper, surrender it to Him, and let Him lead it. The important thing is your intention and action to meet with God.

Personal Reflection: What is God saying to Me?

Proverbs 31:31

Honor her for all that her hands have done, and let her works bring her praise at the city gate.

The Proverbs 31 woman seems impossible, but it is more than just the work she does. In order for her to do the work, she must have character and a certain approach, and because of that, she is respected and praised, and her husband is respected too. You need God to be a godly Proverbs 31 woman. He will develop you and show you how.

Personal Reflection: What is God saying to Me?

Day 184

Psalm 90:17 ESV

Let the favor of the Lord our God be upon us, and establish the work of our hands upon us; yes, establish the work of our hands!

God is a boss. Make no mistake, when God assigns you to His team to work for Him, there is no lounging around, idleness, sleeping in and chilling. No lazy days. God is the best boss but still a boss and will put you to work!

Personal Reflection: What is God saying to Me?

John 18:22-24 NIV

When Jesus said this, one of the officials nearby slapped him in the face. "Is this the way you answer the high priest?" he demanded.

"If I said something wrong," Jesus replied, "testify as to what is wrong. But if I spoke the truth, why did you strike me?" Then Annas sent him bound to Caiaphas, the high priest.

"Ghosts know who to scare," someone once told me. Speak up and use your voice. You train people how to treat you. Speak your truth and let people know it's not okay, and watch them move on to someone else. Don't let Satan intimidate you.

Personal Reflection: What is God saying to Me?

1 Corinthians 9:27

But I discipline my body and keep it under control, lest, after preaching to others I myself should be disqualified.

Discipline in all aspects of being. Begin focusing on the physical, mental, emotional, and spiritual aspects of yourself and spend time devoting to them daily. You need to have a firm handle on them so you can give them over to God. You can't give what you don't have.

Personal Reflection: What is God saying to Me?

Luke 6:37 ESV

Judge not, and you will not be judged; condemn not, and you will not be condemned; forgive, and you will be forgiven.

Forgive. People are not worth the consequences of unforgiveness. I want to be forgiven of my sins by the Lord and I want to have a pure and clean heart. No one is worth me not being seen right in the eyes of the Lord or darkness invading my being. I choose to let it go and forgive.

Personal Reflection: What is God saying to Me?

Proverbs 17:11 ESV

An evil man seeks only rebellion, and a cruel messenger will be sent against him.

Rebellion is not taken lightly by God. What do you think God is doing with your defiance and rebellion? He is not pleased with it, and there will be consequences. Running from God? You will never have peace or rest in rebellion or defiance of God.

Personal Reflection: What is God saying to Me?

2 Corinthians 10:5 ESV

We destroy arguments and every lofty opinion raised against the knowledge of God, and take every thought captive to obey Christ.

Create white space. Spend time to just be. Monitor your thoughts. Know thoughts stir up emotions that you can feel in your skin. Once it is in the body, it is not long before you act. This is how the devil uses you to sin. Mind your thoughts. Resist darkness.

Personal Reflection: What is God saying to Me?

DAY 190

Matthew 22:39 ESV

And a second is like it: You shall love your neighbor *as* yourself.

Stop giving away your power to others that should be given to God. It's okay to say no, not today. It is okay to not answer the phone or respond to the text. You are valuable and worthy. Your feelings, rest, and needs are important too. Let them think what they will about you. They are not your master.

Personal Reflection: What is God saying to Me?

Luke 9:62 ESV

Jesus said to him, "No one who puts his hand to the plow and looks back is fit for the kingdom of God."

No more hard decisions. The decision has already been made to follow God no matter the cost. The only thing left to work out is the logistics, and even that God has covered.

Personal Reflection: What is God saying to Me?

John 15:4 AMPC

Dwell in Me, and I will dwell in you. [Live in Me, and I will live in you.

When you get me, you get God. My life is surrendered to God. In conversation, God will come up, and scripture. God abides in Me and I in Him. Why wouldn't He show up? We are a package deal. Take it or leave it. Do you feel the same?

Personal Reflection: What is God saying to Me?

Day 193

Nehemiah 4:6 NKJV

So we built the wall, and the entire wall was joined together up to half its height, for the people had a mind to work.

Nehemiah was only successful in building the wall because he would not allow himself to be distracted. People were angry, doubtful, envious. They plotted against him, tried to slow him down, desired to intimidate him, but he would not be moved. In this season, resolve not to be moved.

Personal Reflection: What is God saying to Me?

Day 194

Hebrews 12:11 ESV

For the moment, all discipline seems painful rather than pleasant, but later it yields the peaceful fruit of righteousness to those who have been trained by it.

God needs you disciplined. There is so much God desires you to do as an individual, in all your relational roles, for your home, job, ministry, and in your relationship with Him. You will never get it all done unless you submit to Him, are disciplined, and follow His lead.

Personal Reflection: What is God saying to Me?

Joshua 21:43 ESV

Thus the Lord gave to Israel all the land that He swore to give to their fathers. They took possession of it, and they settled there.

Are the walls of Jericho falling down? If so, rejoice! It may feel like all is crumbling, but don't sit amongst the rubble and cry. Instead, see it as the opportunity you need to now step over it and conquer new land. Take your new territory by force.

Personal Reflection: What is God saying to Me?

1 Peter 4:8 NIV

Above all, love each other deeply, because love covers over a multitude of sins.

Lord, make me an instrument of your love. Help me not to be a taker but a giver, a lover not a fighter. Let my love be given without condition.

Personal Reflection: What is God saying to Me?

Matthew 19:26 NIV

Jesus looked at them and said, "With man this is impossible, but with God all things are possible."

God stretches you to what He knows He created you to stretch to, not what you think. He will move you beyond your limits to grow you because He knows you can. He is merely revealing to you what you can do. It's hard; you want to quit, but God knows you can do even more.

Personal Reflection: What is God saying to Me?

Day 198

Ephesians 5:16 ESV

Making the best use of the time, because the days are evil. Therefore do not be foolish, but understand what the will of the Lord is.

God wants you not just effective but efficient. Seek God in your actions in life and in your interactions with others. God knows exactly what needs to be done at any given time and can get to the very seed of the matter. Move not just with impact but without wasting even a moment.

Personal Reflection: What is God saying to Me?

Proverbs 14:12 KJV

There is a way which seemeth right unto a man, but the end thereof are the ways of death.

I'm like many Bible characters—Job, Jonah, Esther, David, Abraham. It simply goes on and on. I wish I would have just had the Solomon experience—straight to the riches—but maybe that's why he ended up the way he did. What character do you resemble?

Personal Reflection: What is God saying to Me?

Matthew 23:12 NIV

For those who exalt themselves will be humbled, and those who humble themselves will be exalted.

Make no mistake, I laid down my life for God. I was too stubbornly resourceful to let God bring me low and strip me to be brought high. I had to partner with God to release and rely on Him for all. Will you partner with God and allow Him to humble you?

Personal Reflection: What is God saying to Me?

James 4:7-8 NCV

So give yourselves completely to God. Stand against the devil, and the devil will run from you.

Come near to God, and God will come near to you.

Go after God with everything you have! Let it look silly, messy. Don't worry about what it looks like or what will happen. Just give God all and watch what He does. He will lead you and guide you. You steps are ordered. He has you.

Personal Reflection: What is God saying to Me?

Micah 6:8 ESV

He has told you, O man, what is good; and what does the Lord require of you but to do justice, and to love kindness, and to walk humbly with your God?

Be in step with God. What is just as bad as not following God and moving when He instructs is going ahead of God and leaving Him behind. God desires you to walk with Him and the devil is looking to separate you. Be cautious. Stick with God.

Personal Reflection: What is God saying to Me?

2 Corinthians 6:14 NIV

Do not be yoked together with unbelievers. For what do righteousness and wickedness have in common? Or what fellowship can light have with darkness?

Why non-Christian friends? Why would you want someone in your inner circle who is a child of Satan? If God is not their Father, who is? If the Holy Spirit is not in them, leading and guiding, what spirit is? Why are you so comfortable around them? Why are they so comfortable around you?

Personal Reflection: What is God saying to Me?

Day 204

Proverbs 11:2 ESV

When pride comes, then comes disgrace, but with the humble is wisdom.

I asked God how to balance humility and boldness. He explained the opposite of humility is arrogance and pride. Humility is neither placing yourself above others nor playing small and shrinking. It is always showing up as your true self in love.

Personal Reflection: What is God saying to Me?

Day 205

Genesis 19:17 ESV

And as they brought them out, one said, "Escape for your life. Do not look back or stop anywhere in the valley. Escape to the hills, lest you be swept away."

Going back is not an option. Today, I decided to move forward, to close all doors to my past, to not go back. There is simply today and my future. God told me there is nothing more that the devil likes than for people to live in and return to yesterday. Only steps forward with God.

Personal Reflection: What is God saying to Me?

Matthew 5:37 NKJV

But let your 'Yes' be 'Yes,' and your 'No,' 'No.'

You can say no, not now, I can't. You do not have to do one more volunteer event, one more errand, one more night doing something you hate to please others. Your opinion, desires, wants, and needs are of value. Take your power back from others. Give the energy you give to them to God.

Personal Reflection: What is God saying to Me?

John 7:24 ESV

Do not judge by appearances, but judge with right judgment."

I will no longer live in lala land, in which I believe everyone is for me. Not everyone has good intentions; not everyone has a good heart, and at any given moment that heart can turn cold. I will trust Jesus and Him alone. All others I will guard my heart.

Personal Reflection: What is God saying to Me?

Isaiah 26:3 ESV

You keep him in perfect peace whose mind is stayed on You, because he trusts in you.

Did you know you don't have to answer the phone or text? You can just not respond to rude people and walk away from that which makes you feel uncomfortable. You can distance yourself from others. Let people know you're not available this season; your focus is on God. Protect your peace.

Personal Reflection: What is God saying to Me?

DAY 209

John 7:37-39 NLT

On the last day, the climax of the festival, Jesus stood and shouted to the crowds, "Anyone who is thirsty may come to me! Anyone who believes in me may come and drink! For the Scriptures declare, 'Rivers of living water will flow from his heart.'" (When he said "living water," he was speaking of the Spirit, who would be given to everyone believing in him. But the Spirit had not yet been given, because Jesus had not yet entered into his glory.)

People should get the overflow from your cup, not what's in your cup. You need to sit at the well of the living water that will never run dry and always fill up. If not, you will fill your cup with things of no permanence. As you pour out, you will never be able to do enough to keep it full.

Personal Reflection: What is God saying to Me?

Philippians 4:19 (ESV)

And my God will supply every need of yours according to His riches in glory in Christ Jesus.

Today, I operate in faith. No matter what, I will trust the Lord. I do not have to see it with my eyes. I do not have to perceive it with my senses. I simply will listen to my Father's instructions and obey. He knows what I stand in need of. If I don't have it, I don't need it.

Personal Reflection: What is God saying to Me?

Joshua 1:9 ESV

Have I not commanded you? Be strong and courageous. Do not be frightened, and do not be dismayed, for the Lord your God is with you wherever you go.

Today, take back territory! Take back your power and do as the Father has told you to do and be who He created you to be.

Personal Reflection: What is God saying to Me?

Day 212

Isaiah 41:10 ESV

Fear not, for I am with you; be not dismayed, for I am your God; I will strengthen you, I will help you, I will uphold you with my righteous right hand.

Fear is not your portion. You will not allow people to push you around. Their opinions will not move you or silence you. Your fear of rejection will not cause you to shrink. Today, you will stand boldly in the fire of the Holy Spirit and be all that God has called you to be.

Personal Reflection: What is God saying to Me?

1 John 4:7-12 ESV

Beloved, let us love one another, for love is from God, and whoever loves has been born of God and knows God. Anyone who does not love does not know God, because God is love. In this the love of God was made manifest among us, that God sent his only Son into the world, so that we might live through him. In this is love, not that we have loved God but that he loved us and sent his Son to be the propitiation for our sins. Beloved, if God so loved us, we also ought to love one another. No one has ever seen God; if we love one another, God abides in us and his love is perfected in us.

Finding it difficult to love? Are you warm, open, inviting, and serving others? Are you that way to God? If you are resistant or rebelling against God, know that you have cut yourself off from the source of love. God is love. Surrender, receive, and release the flow of love in and through you.

Personal Reflection: What is God saying to Me?

Psalm 77:13 NET

O God, your deeds are extraordinary. What god can compare to our great God?

Go for the extraordinary. Don't settle for regular. Tired of feeling bored, stagnant, stuck? Are you waiting for something major to occur? Waiting for the main event in your life? Do you want to see miracles, signs, and wonders? This is what God does!!! Partner with God to receive.

Personal Reflection: What is God saying to Me?

Hebrews 13:2 EHV

Do not fail to show love to strangers, for by doing this some have welcomed angels without realizing it.

Do you know there are angels that walk amongst you? Do you know you have God helpers sent to lead and guide you? Who is here to usher you into your next season? Don't be dismissive of others. Use discernment. Ask God who is for you and who is not. Partner with God. Partner with them.

Personal Reflection: What is God saying to Me?

Acts 20:28 NIV

Keep watch over yourselves and all the flock of which the Holy Spirit has made you overseers. Be shepherds of the church of God, which He bought with His own blood.

Why can't we talk about church issues publicly? It's like we can't tell our dirty laundry. Wash it, don't hide it! Much of the New Testament is spent on church issues. Maybe we can make progress, fill churches, and usher in the new generation if we begin facing the truth, inviting Jesus to transform us into the truth of Himself.

Personal Reflection: What is God saying to Me?

Psalm 63:8 ESV

My soul clings to you; your right hand upholds me.

Choose God this season. Chase Him with all your heart and soul. Put Him over everything and everyone, including yourself. Decide now to break through with God. Watch how exponential your growth and productivity are. Let Him reveal a new you that has partnered with the "I AM."

Personal Reflection: What is God saying to Me?

Isaiah 53:10 KJV

Yet it pleased the Lord to bruise him; He hath put him to grief: when thou shalt make his soul an offering for sin, He shall see his seed, he shall prolong his days, and the pleasure of the Lord shall prosper in his hand.

It pleased the Father that Jesus was bruised and crushed. For God's children, what is crushed is that of flesh which is at enmity with the Father. It's all that holds you back from intimacy with Him and seeking, walking in your identity. He also knows what's on the other side is glory.

Personal Reflection: What is God saying to Me?

Matthew 26:11 NIV

The poor you will always have with you, but you will not always have me.

The need is not the call. Jesus reminds us that we will always have the poor among us but not Him. Don't simply chase needs. Instead, chase the will of the Father.

Personal Reflection: What is God saying to Me?

Ecclesiastes 3:1 ESV

For everything there is a season, and a time for every matter under heaven.

You do not want anything outside God's perfect timing. If you have not received it, it means something else is needed before you get it. You don't want your blessing to become a curse because you were missing one thing. He may need to prepare you it or them. Trust God's wisdom.

Personal Reflection: What is God saying to Me?

Luke 22:42 NIVUK

Father, if you are willing, take this cup from me; yet not my will, but yours be done.

What do you want? What does God want? Are they in alignment with one another? If not, that could be the issue. Take the time to consider both questions. Bring them before the Lord.

Personal Reflection: What is God saying to Me?

Jeremiah 1:4-5 NKJV

Then the word of the Lord came to me, saying: "Before I formed you in the womb I knew you; Before you were born I sanctified you; I ordained you a prophet to the nations."

Read Jeremiah 1. It is what God wants to do with us if we allow Him to. He wants to inform us of who we are, train us, address our fears, encourage and embolden us, instruct us, and then strengthen us. Let God speak to you in this way. Give Him your time.

Personal Reflection: What is God saying to Me?

Day 223

Mark 6:31 WE

Jesus said to them, 'Come away with me. Let us go alone to a quiet place and rest for a while.'

Let God take you on an amazing journey. He got stuff that's not in the book but completely supported by the book. Some things are just wild and extraordinary. It will be unique, and tailor-made just for you to restore and launch you into destiny.

Personal Reflection: What is God saying to Me?

Day 224

Philippians 4:6-7 ESV

Do not be anxious about anything, but in everything by prayer and supplication with thanksgiving let your requests be made known to God. And the peace of God, which surpasses all understanding, will guard your hearts and your minds in Christ Jesus.

I realized people fear the unknown, lack of certainty, instability, and lack of security. We are raised to seek its opposites, and this is why many fear turning to God. God told me He doesn't want people to live this way. He wants people to find safety, security, and certainty in Him.

Personal Reflection: What is God saying to Me?

Proverbs 10:12 ESV

Hatred stirs up strife, but love covers all offenses.

Meeting hate with hate only satisfies Satan. Love and light defeat darkness as it is God Himself. Partner with God and let God shine through.

Personal Reflection: What is God saying to Me?

Luke 6:27 ESV

But I say to you who hear: love your enemies, do good to those who hate you, bless those who curse you, pray for those who abuse you.

Praying for the well-being of my enemies? God explained that I needed to separate the man from Satan's agenda, working through him to hurt me and sow seeds of darkness. When I respond with a desire of ill will, this is not of God's spirit. It is of the enemy.

Personal Reflection: What is God saying to Me?

John 14:6 NIV

Jesus answered, "I am the way and the truth and the life. No one comes to the Father except through me."

Why my God? Jesus is the way, the truth, and the life, and no one comes to the Father but through Him. And my God actually talks back. My God walks with me through this life as Father God, as Jesus Christ, my Lord, friend, and brother. His spirit lives in me. Why, my God? He's real.

Personal Reflection: What is God saying to Me?

Day 228

Matthew 17:20 ESV

He said to them, "Because of your little faith. For truly, I say to you, if you have faith like a grain of mustard seed, you will say to this mountain, 'Move from here to there,' and it will move, and nothing will be impossible for you."

God doesn't need perfect faith. Know that your faith is being perfected. He needs enough faith for you to position yourself for the miracle. What did He tell you to do? Just do it! Scared, fearful, doubtful—just do what He has told you to do so that He can bless you.

Personal Reflection: What is God saying to Me?

Day 229

Matthew 23:10 MSG

And don't let people maneuver you into taking charge of them. There is only one Life-Leader for you and them - Christ. When people show you that they want you to be their everything, what they are showing you is they want Jesus. You cannot be someone's everything. Move out of the way and give them room to seek everything from the one that they need: Jesus. Leave people to Jesus.

Personal Reflection: What is God saying to Me?

Galatians 5:16 ESV

But I say, walk by the Spirit, and you will not gratify the desires of the flesh.

Why do people say they are spiritual? This means they are spirit-filled and spirit-led. If you are not filled and led by the Holy Spirit, what spirit is it? Do not be misled. Salvation comes through Jesus Christ and Him alone. Be led only of the Holy Spirit.

Personal Reflection: What is God saying to Me?

Day 231

Ephesians 4:29-32 ESV

Let no corrupting talk come out of your mouths, but only such as is good for building up, as fits the occasion, that it may give grace to those who hear. And do not grieve the Holy Spirit of God, by whom you were sealed for the day of redemption. Let all bitterness and wrath and anger and clamor and slander be put away from you, along with all malice. Be kind to one another, tenderhearted, forgiving one another, as God in Christ forgave you.

People are often self-focused. They don't care to know how you are doing or about your deepest thoughts and feelings. They desire to serve themselves, and you're not even needed for the conversation. Serve others in conversation and bring your needs and wants to God.

Personal Reflection: What is God saying to Me?

Ecclesiastes 12:7 NKJV

Then the dust will return to the earth as it was, And the spirit will return to God who gave it.

I asked the Lord what happens to the soul when we die, and He told me we didn't need it. Our mind is meant to reason, perceive what was taking place in our external environments; our will would be His and our emotions certainly don't serve us. What happens to the soul? It dies.

Personal Reflection: What is God saying to Me?

Joshua 24:14–15 ESV

Now, therefore, fear the Lord and serve Him in sincerity and in faithfulness. Put away the gods that your fathers served beyond the River and in Egypt, and serve the Lord. And if it is evil in your eyes to serve the Lord, choose this day whom you will serve, whether the gods your fathers served in the region beyond the River, or the gods of the Amorites in whose land you dwell. But as for me and my house, we will serve the Lord.

I asked the Lord why the devil exists. He said it was to provide an alternative. He did not want to force His children or angels to serve Him. Choose this day whom you will serve? Choosing self is a choice that follows in the pattern of Satan. It is a choice to follow Him.

Personal Reflection: What is God saying to Me?

Day 234

Deuteronomy 31:8 ESV

It is the Lord who goes before you. He will be with you; He will not leave you or forsake you. Do not fear or be dismayed.

God, I trust you with my life. I trust you with things I don't understand, things I am resistant to. I trust the path you have set before me, no matter how impossible it looks or scary it may seem. I know that as long as you have led me, you will be present with me and see me through.

Personal Reflection: What is God saying to Me?

Psalms 27:14 AMP

Wait for and confidently expect the LORD; Be strong and let your heart take courage; Yes, wait for and confidently expect the LORD.

God told me that what I lacked was not faith or works. Not time spent, not intimacy, not good intention. I lacked the willingness to wait on God. To be still. If I was not hard at work, I would quit as there was no progress. He wants to show me the much He can do with my little.

Personal Reflection: What is God saying to Me?

Psalm 95:6 ESV

Oh come, let us worship and bow down; let us kneel before the Lord, our Maker!

How do we meet God in worship? We must separate worship from song. It's more. Its praise and adoration and song is a tool. When people do so with the intent to give their all to God, they open their hearts, and this is His invitation to come in to sup with them.

Personal Reflection: What is God saying to Me?

Galatians 2:20 ASV

I have been crucified with Christ; and it is no longer I that live, but Christ liveth in me: and that life which I now live in the flesh I live in faith, the faith which is in the Son of God, who loved me, and gave himself up for me.

God desires me to offer my body as a living sacrifice so the He may make His home there and operate through it. He wants it for Himself to live in this world. He wants us to die so in Him we may live.

Personal Reflection: What is God saying to Me?

Isaiah 42:6 BBE

6 I the Lord have made you the vessel of my purpose, I have taken you by the hand, and kept you safe, and I have given you to be an agreement to the people, and a light to the nations:

God really wants to us me a vessel for His glory. This is why I needed to surrender, obey, sacrifice, love, have faith and trust. He wants me to deny myself, put myself aside so He can use me. No, not tell me what to do but move through me.

Personal Reflection: What is God saying to Me?

Proverbs 28:26 ESV

Whoever trusts in his own mind is a fool, but he who walks in wisdom will be delivered.

I questioned God's love, motives, ways with me. I poured it out. Real, harsh, vulnerable honest, heavy. God took all of that and provided clarity, understanding. Not a way out, but what was needed for a way through. God can handle your worst and use it to turn you into His best.

Personal Reflection: What is God saying to Me?

Matthew 5:16 ESV

In the same way, let your light shine before others, so that they may see your good works and give glory to your Father who is in heaven.

God is using my conversations with Him to show other people what a relationship with God is like to inspire them to have their own relationship with Him. Think of a new way to evangelize. Not through lofty creative speeches or pamphlets but by following God and inspiring others.

Personal Reflection: What is God saying to Me?

Matthew 28:19 NIV

19 Therefore go and make disciples of all nations,

God spoke to me and said I died to reconcile those to God. You, as My disciple, are following in my steps as you have died to self and are making disciples of others. You are not amassing good, loyal church members but followers of Christ. This is how you evangelize.

Personal Reflection: What is God saying to Me?

Mark 16:15-16 ESV

And he said to them, "Go into all the world and proclaim the gospel to the whole creation. Whoever believes and is baptized will be saved, but whoever does not believe will be condemned.

I asked God about how I am evangelizing with my message of take up your cross and follow God while not being in the church. He said that "many churches get people to follow them not Me. You are operating within the body of Christ- My church to bring people directly to Me."

Personal Reflection: What is God saying to Me?

Day 243

2 Corinthians 3:3 ESV

And you show that you are a letter from Christ delivered by us, written not with ink but with the Spirit of the living God, not on tablets of stone but on tablets of human hearts.

God spent so much time teaching, training, and pouring into me. He made me a book! He wrote on the tablet of my heart and then told me to reveal it to others. He sends people to me so that He can write on the tablets of their heart for others to read them. God is the best author.

Personal Reflection: What is God saying to Me?

Galatians 5:1 CSB

1 Christ has liberated us into freedom. Therefore stand firm and don't submit again to a yoke of slavery.

God liberated me from a church not for me, the world, from man and myself. He broke off the control manipulation of man, the fear of the world, and limiting beliefs of myself. This is freedom in Christ. I am now able to be all that God has intended me to be. Go after freedom. Go after Jesus. Let Him then place you where He desires.

Personal Reflection: What is God saying to Me?

2 Corinthians 11:3 ESV

But I am afraid that as the serpent deceived Eve by his cunning, your thoughts will be led astray from a sincere and pure devotion to Christ.

Be cautious. Don't look for the obvious evil. Look for the distraction!

Personal Reflection: What is God saying to Me?

2 Corinthians 2:11 ESV

So that we would not be outwitted by Satan; for we are not ignorant of his designs.

Has someone given up on life and now is placing such a demand on you that it requires your life to keep them afloat? Do you feel heavy, low when you are around them? Know, the devil uses your kind heart to slow down your momentum and stop you from moving in the things of God.

Personal Reflection: What is God saying to Me?

Philippians 4:8 NLT

8 And now, dear brothers and sisters, one final thing. Fix your thoughts on what is true, and honorable, and right, and pure, and lovely, and admirable. Think about things that are excellent and worthy of praise.

Are your dark thoughts constant. Know you are being afflicted by darkness. Resist those thoughts. Invite God in to give you strategy. Eventually, they will slow then they will stop.

Personal Reflection: What is God saying to Me?

Philippians 2:5 ESV

Have this mind among yourselves, which is yours in Christ Jesus

Do you wake up thinking negative thoughts, hateful dark thoughts? Satan has gotten up early to sow seeds of darkness. Who or what is it that you are thinking negatively about? That could be the key because if you could ever get on one accord with it, it could unlock your destiny.

Personal Reflection: What is God saying to Me?

Colossians 3:3 ESV

For you have died, and your life is hidden with Christ in God.

Give up the little you created complete with all of it vanities, ego, self-ambition and self-worship for the You God knew of you when he formed you. Stop living in a false identity the world gives and shapes. Seek Christ for your true identity that is hidden in Him.

Personal Reflection: What is God saying to Me?

Ephesians 3:20 ESV

Now to him who is able to do far more abundantly than all that we ask or think, according to the power at work within us,

If you have a song, a thought, a task that comes up don't hesitate to act on it. Don't suppress or ignore it. It is God's who is providing the inspiration and instruction to move. This wave of inspiration has God's glory on it. Ride the wave of God's glory.

Personal Reflection: What is God saying to Me?

Matthew 6:33 ESV

But seek first the kingdom of God and his righteousness, and all these things will be added to you.

God was teaching me during my workout. After making over 12 videos during my run, he showed me that if I put His business first, my business would still get done only I will have obeyed Him. I trusted that it would get done and if it didn't then I didn't need it. Turned out to be the best workout of my life.

Personal Reflection: What is God saying to Me?

John 1:16 ESV

And from his fullness we have all received, grace upon grace.

If you are frustrated with not receiving a particular blessing, consider all the ways that you are currently being blessed behind the scenes that you are unaware of. You may be fixated on a particular blessing while standing in the midst of many blessings. Thank God.

Personal Reflection: What is God saying to Me?

Galatians 1:10 NKJV

10 For do I now persuade men, or God? Or do I seek to please men? For if I still pleased men, I would not be a bondservant of Christ.

Do not ask man for permission, seek it from God. Stop giving God the authority that belongs to Jesus Christ alone. If God says it is so, let it be so. You will not have to worry about it being shaky, temporary. It will be solid and eternal.

Personal Reflection: What is God saying to Me?

Zechariah 4:6 AMP

'Not by might, nor by power, but by My Spirit

Stop overthinking, over analyzing, stressing about what God has called you to. Don't trust and believe in yourself if you can't. Place it all on God's ability to show up in and through you. Get out of Gods way. God is waiting for you to step aside so His glory can be on display through you.

Personal Reflection: What is God saying to Me?

DAY 255
Psalm 28:7 NKJV

The Lord is my strength and my shield; My heart trusted in Him, and I am helped; Therefore my heart greatly rejoices, And with my song I will praise Him.

Trust God to do not what you would do or what you think He should do but trust Him to do whatever is necessary to bring you to His expected end. You cry out for change but when the change places a demand on you, you cry out for the demand to stop. Let go, Embrace discomfort, trust.

Personal Reflection: What is God saying to Me?

1 Corinthians 3:7 ESV

So neither he who plants nor he who waters is anything, but only God who gives the growth.

Don't just throw scripture at people. Didn't Jesus spend time telling others Sabbath was not Lord over Him, but He is Lord over the Sabbath; the adulterous woman that required death-mercy. Ask people what is God telling them to do? Encourage them to follow God, not you.

Personal Reflection: What is God saying to Me?

DAY 257

Genesis 12:2-3 MSG

I'll make you a great nation and bless you. I'll make you famous; you'll be a blessing. I'll bless those who bless you; those who curse you I'll curse. All the families of the Earth will be blessed through you."

Consider the great promise of Abraham. What is your promise? Live into it. Do not ever get small so others can get big. Don't ever come down from where you are to bring others up. Don't ever go low to bring others up high. Require people to come up to where you are. This is how you truly help people while also maintaining your own trajectory and movement into your promise.

Personal Reflection: What is God saying to Me?

DAY 258

Ephesians 3:17-19 NLT

17 Then Christ will make his home in your hearts as you trust in him. Your roots will grow down into God's love and keep you strong. 18 And may you have the power to understand, as all God's people should, how wide, how long, how high, and how deep his love is. 19 May you experience the love of Christ, though it is too great to understand fully. Then you will be made complete with all the fullness of life and power that comes from God.

God wants to abide in you and you in Him. He wants to make His home with you. God doesn't want to be looked at as a burden, nuisance or worse- a threat, the enemy. He wants to be a Father and Jesus, a friend and brother. Let Him express Himself in new fresh ways through the unique vessel that is you.

Personal Reflection: What is God saying to Me?

James 4:7 KJ21

Submit yourselves therefore to God. Resist the devil, and he will flee from you.

The devil is able to do so much damage in your life because you are allowing Him to. He knows that you will only try to resist but eventually you will break. Today, take your stand and after you have done all you can to stand...stand. Stand in your authority in Jesus Christ.

Personal Reflection: What is God saying to Me?

Day 260

Colossians 3:2 ESV

Set your minds on things that are above, not on things that are on earth.

God told me this was a voicemail and text message season. There is restricted access to me. If you desire to speak to me. Leave a message. I will not be interrupted. I will no longer be at anyone's beck and call. The Lord has business for me and this season I'm about it.

Personal Reflection: What is God saying to Me?

Day 261

Jeremiah 33:3 NKJV

Call to me and I will answer you, and will tell you great and hidden things that you have not known.

Consider how God spoke to Elijah, Moses, Noah, Jonah, Jeremiah, Abraham, Job. Think about how Jesus spoke to Saul. The problem isn't that God doesn't speak to man. Does He not speak to you or are you simply not listening? Give Him time to speak to you. Seek His voice Listen, Obey.

Personal Reflection: What is God saying to Me?

Galatians 5:24 KJ21

And those who are Christ's have crucified the flesh with its affections and lusts.

Look for the opportunity to crucify your flesh; to push past negative feelings; to confront difficult issues. Do not see discomfort as burdens or reasons to not do something. See it as an opportunity for change. Let it challenge you into digging deep exploring new aspects of you.

Personal Reflection: What is God saying to Me?

Hebrews 12:1 ESV

Therefore, since we are surrounded by so great a cloud of witnesses, let us also lay aside every weight, and sin which clings so closely, and let us run with endurance the race that is set before us,

Get rid of anything that stands in the way of your intimacy with God. Remove all barriers that hinder you from reaching your destiny. No longer tolerate anything that keeps you from your Father and all that He has created you to be.

Personal Reflection: What is God saying to Me?

1 Thessalonians 2:4 ESV

But just as we have been approved by God to be entrusted with the gospel, so we speak, not to please man, but to please God who tests our hearts.

No more fake nice, not standing in your authority and speaking truth. Be silent out of wisdom, not out of fear. Shrinking, people pleasing, fear of man is not Christian. Christ said whatever was necessary in truth to reconcile those to God. Can God trust you to do the same.

Personal Reflection: What is God saying to Me?

Psalm 139:7-10 ESV

Where shall I go from your Spirit? Or where shall I flee from your presence? If I ascend to heaven, you are there! If I make my bed in Sheol, you are there! If I take the wings of the morning and dwell in the uttermost parts of the sea, even there your hand shall lead me, and your right hand shall hold me.

All of that energy we spend running from God, avoiding, delaying, hesitating is fruitless. It produces no benefit and sometimes devastating results. Why not have a change of heart and turn to God? Run to Him. Run with Him and produce good fruit.

Personal Reflection: What is God saying to Me?

1 Corinthians 3:9 ESV

For we are God's fellow workers. You are God's field, God's building.

God is doing so much more than you could imagine in your life. He works behind the scenes blocking evil, setting up opportunities, improving and removing relationships. He is leading you to the Way. Don't leave God to work your life alone. Work with God. Let the transformation begin.

Personal Reflection: What is God saying to Me?

James 1:22-25 ESV

But be doers of the word, and not hearers only, deceiving yourselves. For if anyone is a hearer of the word and not a doer, he is like a man who looks intently at his natural face in a mirror. For he looks at himself and goes away and at once forgets what he was like. But the one who looks into the perfect law, the law of liberty, and perseveres, being no hearer who forgets but a doer who acts, he will be blessed in his doing.

Stop being lazy. Stop being so casual with your Christian walk. Satan is having a field day with our inconsistency. One day God's, one day his. Base your walk on your feelings- your walk will be fickle, wishy washy, unreliable. Stop playing with God. Take God off pause and COMMIT.

Personal Reflection: What is God saying to Me?

Isaiah 43:1 ESV

But now thus says the Lord, he who created you, O Jacob, he who formed you, O Israel: "Fear not, for I have redeemed you; I have called you by name, you are mine.

What makes me worthy of God? I run, quit, give up when things get hard. I need to be fed-my ego always. I am so limited. I am emotional. God assured me if I would simply give Him the me I created He would transform me into the Me He created. I AM worthy because I AM His.

Personal Reflection: What is God saying to Me?

Matthew 6:10 ESV

Your kingdom come, your will be done, on earth as it is in heaven.

My prayers needed to shift from remove, stop, release to help to endure, strength, understanding and strategy. He is a real Father that will do what is necessary to get me to destiny. My prayer He works daily, "Not my will but your will be done."

Personal Reflection: What is God saying to Me?

DAY 270

Matthew 7:13-14 GNT

Go in through the narrow gate, because the gate to hell is wide and the road that leads to it is easy, and there are many who travel it. 14But the gate to life is narrow and the way that leads to it is hard, and there are few people who find it.

God let me know He has all my prayers, but I needed to change my prayers. The road is narrow, hard and few are on it. The road will not change due to my discomfort. Instead, I needed to trust Him with the path He created and straightens just for me.

Personal Reflection: What is God saying to Me?

Deuteronomy 28:12 NKJV

The LORD will open to you His good treasure, the heavens, to give the rain to your land in its season, and to bless all the work of your hand.

God is not asking for you to do it all. He is asking for you to step, move, walk with Him. God will do the heavy lifting behind the scenes. He will take your little and make much out of it. Your little with God's grace and favor is unimaginable. Let Him WOW you.

Personal Reflection: What is God saying to Me?

Day 272

Proverbs 16:9 ESV

The heart of man plans his way, but the Lord establishes his steps.

What God will do you with your little. Overwhelmed with the magnitude of possibility? Simply take the small step you know to take, and God will order the next one. Make a small move and God will push it into position. Make the little change and God will provide the transformation.

Personal Reflection: What is God saying to Me?

James 4:4 NKJV

Do you not know that friendship with the world is enmity with God? Whoever therefore wants to be a friend of the world makes himself an enemy of God.

Do you desire the world? Just as a mistress is not the answer in a marriage the world is not. Turn back to your first love. Don't just do a bunch of activities. Turn your heart back to the Lord. Open it back up. Establish intimacy with Him, work through your issues and commit.

Personal Reflection: What is God saying to Me?

1 Peter 5:7 ESV

Casting all your anxieties on him, because he cares for you

Desire weed (or _fill in the blank_)? What is your heart's posture? Do you want peace, rest, less anxiety and stress? Know these are all things you should seek Jesus for. Have you come under the power of it? Can you go a day without it, without Jesus? Put the Lord in the place of #1. Seek Him first and weed will fall away.

Personal Reflection: What is God saying to Me?

Isaiah 30:21 ESV

And your ears shall hear a word behind you, saying, "This is the way, walk in it," when you turn to the right or when you turn to the left.

Who is leading your evangelistic efforts? Is it the holy spirit? Satan will push you to do God stuff without God. Wait for God to give you the specific words, message, actions to turn someone's soul to Him. Be led of the spirit to convict and deliver souls not by self-ambition.

Personal Reflection: What is God saying to Me?

Hebrews 11:6 ESV

And without faith it is impossible to please him, for whoever would draw near to God must believe that he exists and that he rewards those who seek him.

Live a life that demands faith. Do you wake up seeking and depending on God? Do you need God to get through your day? If not, how? Are you leaning into the bigness, the greatness, the new thing that cant be imagined that God has for you in all areas of your life? If not seek it, hope for it, depend on God for it.

Personal Reflection: What is God saying to Me?

Day 277

1 Corinthians 14:33 KJV

For God is not the author of confusion, but of peace, as in all churches of the saints.

Prophets should not make up your communication with God. There will be seasons where God will call you away from using others and will call you unto Himself alone. Just as God rises up those to speak to you so does the devil. This could cause confusion. Seek God first.

Personal Reflection: What is God saying to Me?

John 6:63 ESV

It is the Spirit who gives life; the flesh is no help at all. The words that I have spoken to you are spirit and life.

Prophetic words, spiritual leaders, Christian voices are an amazing resource to confirm Gods word for you. God will use them as a tool to give language to what you are going through, provide instruction, encourage you and much more. But know this is only used as a supplement.

Personal Reflection: What is God saying to Me?

Isaiah 9:6 ESV

For to us a child is born, to us a son is given; and the government shall be upon his shoulder, and his name shall be called Wonderful Counselor, Mighty God, Everlasting Father, Prince of Peace.

Our Lord is the Wonderful Counselor. He is the best therapist. He will help you expose your trauma, work through them and heal your soul wounds. Crystals etc. are nothing in comparison to the healing powers of Christ. Put your faith not in the world's creation but in the Creator.

Personal Reflection: What is God saying to Me?

2 Corinthians 11:14 AMP

And no wonder, since Satan himself masquerades as an angel of light.

Be careful not to only look for obvious opposition, evil, darkness. The devil masquerades as an angel of light. Be wise as serpents. Behold! I send you out as sheep amongst the wolves. He could be using the bible, religion to gain access to you through others and your thoughts to do His darkest work in your life.

Personal Reflection: What is God saying to Me?

John 13:34 ESV

A new commandment I give to you, that you love one another: just as I have loved you, you also are to love one another.

I asked God to help me love others. His response was "Jennifer, how do I love you? Love them like that. Evangelize not by fancy speeches or persuasive arguments but by loving them. By giving them love, you give them Me. Make them crave the love. Make them crave Me."

Personal Reflection: What is God saying to Me?

Matthew 4:1-11 NKJV

4 Then Jesus was led up by the Spirit into the wilderness to be tempted by the devil. 2 And when He had fasted forty days and forty nights, afterward He was hungry. 3 Now when the tempter came to Him, he said, "If You are the Son of God, command that these stones become bread..."

Satan spoke to me three times during this walk. He made offers, threats, and instruction to leave God. To my surprise, the voice sounded like my own. Be careful Satan speaks to you more than you think.

Personal Reflection: What is God saying to Me?

Day 283

1 Thessalonians 3:5 ESV

For this reason, when I could bear it no longer, I sent to learn about your faith, for fear that somehow the tempter had tempted you and our labor would be in vain.

Satan spoke to me three times in my processing journey with God. 1)the offer; 2) his fulfillment of unleashing hell 3) at my worst- His receipt of my call and his instruction to denounce God publicly. As you get to know God, you will also get to know Satan. Be prepared. Resist. Cry out to God.

Personal Reflection: What is God saying to Me?

Matthew 22:37 ESV

And he said to him, "You shall love the Lord your God with all your heart and with all your soul and with all your mind. This is the great and first commandment.

The Lord has been knocking at the door of your heart but you will not respond. So, He has recruited me. And because I have allowed Him to make His home with Me, He will enter your heart through me. Don't give others what belongs to Christ. Give Him your time and worship. Give Him you.

Personal Reflection: What is God saying to Me?

1 John 3:8 ESV

Whoever makes a practice of sinning is of the devil, for the devil has been sinning from the beginning. The reason the Son of God appeared was to destroy the works of the devil.

Do not play with sin. God is not to be left on pause. Satan does not want you to rest, have fun, be free, he wants you dead. He will oppress you into thoughts of depression, hopelessness, insanity, and suicide. He wants you as an instrument of sin or worse, dead by your own hands.

Personal Reflection: What is God saying to Me?

Joshua 23:8 NLT

8 Rather, cling tightly to the Lord your God as you have done until now.

Is all hell breaking loose in your life? You might be in training. God will pull his hand back and allow Satan to wreak havoc in your life to train you to cling to Him, spiritually war, wait on Him, humble yourself and practice spiritual disciplines. You are safely in God's hands.

Personal Reflection: What is God saying to Me?

Isaiah 64:8 ESV

But now, O Lord, you are our Father; we are the clay, and you are our potter; we are all the work of your hand.

Why rock bottom? At rock bottom we have pushed past the limits of what we can do. We have gone beyond ourselves, and God can do the work of rebuilding. We are moldable, shapeable, pliable for the Potter. Jesus was crucified and now is at the right hand of the Father. It is a set up.

Personal Reflection: What is God saying to Me?

Romans 12:4 ESV

For as in one body we have many members, and the members do not all have the same function,

There is a season for everything. Whether it be building, transition, relationship building, processing etc. Make sure you know that everyone's walk is different. It is all according to God's time. Be ok where God has you. Define success not by human standards but by following God.

Personal Reflection: What is God saying to Me?

2 Corinthians 10:4

New Living Translation

4 We use God's mighty weapons, not worldly weapons, to knock down the strongholds of human reasoning and to destroy false arguments.

Partner with God. God is undefeated. Do not try to fight Satan alone. You are no match for him. He responds not to motivation, courage, boldness, change of routines, sage, meditation. He responds to the authority of Jesus Christ. Get to Jesus.

Personal Reflection: What is God saying to Me?

Day 290

Galatians 5:7 NLT

You were running the race so well. Who has held you back from following the truth?

What did you long for before you came to Christ? Remember when you were desperate for Him and hungered for Him? Did you get what you were looking for? What happened? Who or what cut in on the good race you were running? Go back to your first love. Fall in love again.

Personal Reflection: What is God saying to Me?

Day 291

Matthew 11:28-30 MSG

28-30 "Are you tired? Worn out? Burned out on religion? Come to me. Get away with me and you'll recover your life. I'll show you how to take a real rest. Walk with me and work with me—watch how I do it. Learn the unforced rhythms of grace. I won't lay anything heavy or ill-fitting on you. Keep company with me and you'll learn to live freely and lightly."

Do you want to reach new spiritual heights and make new discoveries in the spiritual realm? Step out of tradition and religion. Throw out the checklist and go away with God. He wants people who will not restrict Him but will allow Him to reveal Himself to you and your true self to you.

Personal Reflection: What is God saying to Me?

2 Corinthians 10:5 ESV

We destroy arguments and every lofty opinion raised against the knowledge of God, and take every thought captive to obey Christ,

Don't accept negative emotions that pull you away from God. Any dark emotion or feeling that keeps you from seeking God or moving toward purpose or destiny is of your adversary the devil. Laziness, depression, malaise, boredom, apathy, despondency, suicidal ideation are all the enemy.

Personal Reflection: What is God saying to Me?

1 Kings 8:17-19 MSG

"My father David had it in his heart to build a Temple honoring the Name of GOD, the God of Israel. But GOD told him 'It was good that you wanted to build a Temple in my honor—most commendable! But you are not the one to do it—your son will build it to honor my Name.

Christianity is not just about doing good; it is about doing God. David desired to build a house for the Lord. It was good. It was God but it was not for Him, it was for his son. You can get wrapped up into doing good and completely miss out on the reason why you were created.

Personal Reflection: What is God saying to Me?

Proverbs 25:28 ESV

A man without self-control is like a city broken into and left without walls.

"Feelings are terrible masters but great servants". Do you know you could have the worse feelings and still do what God tells you to do? You don't have to feel great or even called. You simply need to do what God says. Why? Because why call Him Lord, Lord it you will not obey? Keep Jesus as Lord and not your feelings.

Personal Reflection: What is God saying to Me?

Jeremiah 10:23 ESV

I know, O Lord, that the way of man is not in himself, that it is not in man who walks to direct his steps.

God is using me to show others what a relationship with Him looks like beyond tradition and religion. He desires people to know that the makeup of the Christian walk is -Follow God; To take up your cross and Follow Him and to show you what He will do when you take the limits off.

Personal Reflection: What is God saying to Me?

Joel 2:12 NIV

12 "Even now," declares the Lord, "return to me with all your heart, with fasting and weeping and mourning."

Today I was brought to my lowest ever in my walk. Rock bottom. There was no lower. I turned, only for a moment, but I gave up and turned. Satan and I again had a conversation. I needed to repent and ask for forgiveness. Know you are never too far gone, and it is never too late.

Personal Reflection: What is God saying to Me?

Romans 3:23 NKJV

23 for all have sinned and fall short of the glory of God,

Even in my rebellion, God was teaching. The lesson- get "into the perfect will of God" out of your vocabulary. Everyone falls short-even you. If not, people will inevitably falter and then turn from me because they will consider themselves unworthy. This is not perfection. It's a covenant.

Personal Reflection: What is God saying to Me?

Psalm 139:13-14 ESV

For you formed my inward parts; you knitted me together in my mother's womb. I praise you, for I am fearfully and wonderfully made. Wonderful are your works; my soul knows it very well.

God has something uniquely for you that goes beyond typical roles. Don't settle for average, ordinary, mundane, safe, secure. Seek God for the great purpose He has for you. Abandon all reason as you Follow God.

Personal Reflection: What is God saying to Me?

Galatians 1:15-17

15 But even before I was born, God chose me and called me by his marvelous grace. Then it pleased him 16 to reveal his Son to me[e] so that I would proclaim the Good News about Jesus to the Gentiles.

When this happened, I did not rush out to consult with any human being. 17 Nor did I go up to Jerusalem to consult with those who were apostles before I was.

Do not rely on other people to inform, validate, support who you are in Christ. You are not waiting on the opportunity from man, you are waiting on God's timing. Men should not size you up and direct your steps. God has an identity for you and will order your steps. Seek Him.

Personal Reflection: What is God saying to Me?

Hebrews 12:1 AMP

Therefore, since we are surrounded by so great a cloud of witnesses [who by faith have testified to the truth of God's absolute faithfulness], stripping off every unnecessary weight and the sin which so easily and cleverly entangles us, let us run with endurance and active persistence the race that is set before us,

Let go of the weight that so besets you. Is it a person, a thing, a place? Let it go and watch yourself soar to new heights. Don't let it drag you down. Do not carry deadweight. Release it. Follow God and Free people to seek God to.

Personal Reflection: What is God saying to Me?

Day 301

John 14:6 NIV

6 Jesus answered, "I am the way and the truth and the life. No one comes to the Father except through me.

Trust God. He knows the truth about the way to life. It's Him. Let Him reveal Himself to you.

Personal Reflection: What is God saying to Me?

Psalms 62:5-8 The Message MSG

God, the one and only— I'll wait as long as he says. Everything I hope for comes from him, so why not? He's solid rock under my feet, breathing room for my soul, An impregnable castle: I'm set for life. My help and glory are in God —granite-strength and safe-harbor-God— So trust him absolutely, people; lay your lives on the line for him. God is a safe place to be.

Chasing man will only get you so far. Chasing God will run you into destiny. Just for a season take your focus off of being pleasing to man; to be viewed as acceptable in the eyes of man and shift it to being right in the eyes of God. Embrace His will and watch your whole life change.

Personal Reflection: What is God saying to Me?

DAY 303

Galatians 2:20 ESV

I have been crucified with Christ. It is no longer I who live, but Christ who lives in me. And the life I now live in the flesh I live by faith in the Son of God, who loved me and gave himself for me.

Are you crucified with Christ or being crucified with Christ? Do you still want, need, desire? Dead men don't. Give them over to the Lord. Detach from them and let Him give you the desires of your heart and supply all of your needs according to His riches and glory.

Personal Reflection: What is God saying to Me?

Isaiah 41:13 NIV

"For I am the Lord your God who takes hold of your right hand and says to you, Do not fear; I will help you."

Do it anyway. Do it not wanting to, not being motivated to, fearful, not knowing what to do, not having resources. Just get it done. Your destiny does not require good feelings, it requires you to show up and do the work.

Personal Reflection: What is God saying to Me?

Hebrews 12:2 ESV

Looking to Jesus, the founder and perfecter of our faith, who for the joy that was set before him endured the cross, despising the shame, and is seated at the right hand of the throne of God.

Abraham did not display perfect Faith. He birthed Ishmael with a slave, laughed when God told Him he would still have a son, deceived kings. Why did the promise take so long, almost decades? His faith was being perfected, so is yours.

Personal Reflection: What is God saying to Me?

1 Corinthians 12:7-11 NIV

7 Now to each one the manifestation of the Spirit is given for the common good. 8 To one there is given through the Spirit a message of wisdom, to another a message of knowledge by means of the same Spirit, 9 to another faith by the same Spirit, to another gifts of healing by that one Spirit, 10 to another miraculous powers, to another prophecy, to another distinguishing between spirits, to another speaking in different kinds of tongues,[a] and to still another the interpretation of tongues. 11 All these are the work of one and the same Spirit, and he distributes them to each one, just as he determines.

Can God get access to His church? They are controlled by men who manipulate, politic, take advantage. They stronghold ministry and God can't breathe on His church and perform miracles signs and wonders. Let people be used of God in your church to behold the new thing god is doing.

Personal Reflection: What is God saying to Me?

Isaiah 26:3 ESV

You keep him in perfect peace whose mind is stayed on you, because he trusts in you

Do not allow your thoughts to roam free. Whenever you have thoughts contrary to that of the spirit of God, resist and they will flee. Interrupt the thought with this quick prayer:

" Lord,
I Give this __(negative emotion)_ over to you.
I CAST it over to you.
It does not SERVE me or the purpose you have for me.
The BATTLE is not Mine. It is yours.
I TRUST you with it"

Personal Reflection: What is God saying to Me?

Matthew 16:23 BSB

22 Peter took Him aside and began to rebuke Him. "Far be it from You, Lord!" he said. "This shall never happen to You!" 23But Jesus turned and said to Peter, "Get behind Me, Satan! You are a stumbling block to Me.

Evaluate the difficult relationship you have been in for years. If I said it was demonic in nature would that explain everything. If so, bring that person before the Lord and ask for strategy.

Personal Reflection: What is God saying to Me?

1 Kings 17:2 NIV

2 Then the word of the Lord came to Elijah: 3 "Leave here, turn eastward and hide in the Kerith Ravine, east of the Jordan. 4 You will drink from the brook, and I have directed the ravens to supply you with food there."

The Lord provided supernaturally in my time of need. There is no way to explain it. I was discouraged by my situation but it was exactly where He placed me so He could show me another way of living. Trust God.

Personal Reflection: What is God saying to Me?

1 Thessalonians 2:18 NIV

For we wanted to come to you—certainly I, Paul, did, again and again—but Satan blocked our way.

God gave me a football field analogy. Realize, you have opponents that are working on defense to keep you from getting to the other side. Partner with God. He invented the game, and it is all subject to His authority. He can help you run into your destiny. Trust Him.

Personal Reflection: What is God saying to Me?

Psalm 16:11 ESV

You make known to me the path of life; in your presence there is fullness of joy; at your right hand are pleasures forevermore.

Life gets good when you start following God. Not because you have a lot but because you Have Him and that's more than enough. Go get your joy back!!

Personal Reflection: What is God saying to Me?

DAY 312

Isaiah 55:11 AMP

So will My word be which goes out of My mouth; It will not return to Me void (useless, without result), Without accomplishing what I desire, And without succeeding in the matter for which I sent it.

What do you think God is doing with your no or even hesitancy?

1-Nevermind;

2-I'll wait;

3-Now.

At whatever cost, God's word does not return void. He watches over it to make sure it is fulfilled no matter the cost. He will respond to your no as He did Jonah and even Jacob. He will create or allow hardship or wrestle with your flesh to subdue it. If you are having troubles in your life or in your very soul, bring that before the Lord so he can provide clarity and understanding. Then obey.

Personal Reflection: What is God saying to Me?

Philippians 4:13 ESV

I can do all things through him who strengthens me.
    Steps are revealed as you take them. Take the step.

Personal Reflection: What is God saying to Me?

Hebrews 9:28 ESV

So Christ, having been offered once to bear the sins of many, will appear a second time, not to deal with sin but to save those who are eagerly waiting for him.

Jesus is coming back. The time is now. Get to know Jesus while there is still time.

Personal Reflection: What is God saying to Me?

Romans 11:29 ESV

For the gifts and the calling of God are irrevocable.
    God is calling you. Answer the call.

Personal Reflection: What is God saying to Me?

Day 316

Ephesians 4:22-24 GNT

22 So get rid of your old self, which made you live as you used to—the old self that was being destroyed by its deceitful desires. 23 Your hearts and minds must be made completely new, 24 and you must put on the new self, which is created in God's likeness and reveals itself in the true life that is upright and holy.

Let go of the old! Make room for the new. God has not given you the new because He knows you are still attached to the old. So, when things get rocky, uncomfortable, unfamiliar you will discard the new and simply go back to the old. Release the old and watch God work.

Personal Reflection: What is God saying to Me?

Hebrews 4:16 NKJV

16 Let us therefore come boldly to the throne of grace, that we may obtain mercy and find grace to help in time of need

Go boldly to the throne of God and make your request? Know you are talking to the I AM that I AM and the there is nothing too hard for Him. Press in but be willing to say, not my will but your will be done.

Personal Reflection: What is God saying to Me?

Isaiah 1:19 ESV

If you are willing and obedient, you shall eat the good of the land;
Are you ready for that prayer to be answered right now? Have you done everything God has asked you to do; everything you know to do? Have you positioned yourself to receive the miracle? If not, you are not waiting on God. God is waiting on you. Move.

Personal Reflection: What is God saying to Me?

Day 319

Romans 12:3 AMP

For by the grace [of God] given to me I say to everyone of you not to think more highly of himself [and of his importance and ability] than he ought to think; but to think so as to have sound judgment, as God has apportioned to each a degree of faith [and a purpose designed for service].

I am thankful that we do not have to go through life alone, that the Lord desires to walk with us. I can take credit for nothing. Even my measure of faith is a gift from God. He is able and through Him so am I.

Personal Reflection: What is God saying to Me?

Psalm 18:16 ESV

He sent from on high, he took me; he drew me out of many waters.

The Bible says Satan kills, steals and destroys. It also says he roams around like a roaring Lion seeking whom he can devour. How is he doing this in your life? Know your enemy. Ask God for strategy.

Personal Reflection: What is God saying to Me?

Colossians 3:2 ESV

Set your minds on things that are above, not on things that are on earth.

However, you are feeling this morning, do what the Lord is telling you to do. The work doesn't require your good feelings. It just wants to get done. The checklist at the end of the day requires a checkmark, not good vibes. Place your feelings at the feet of Jesus, then get moving.

Personal Reflection: What is God saying to Me?

1 John 3:1 ESV

See what kind of love the Father has given to us, that we should be called children of God; and so we are. The reason why the world does not know us is that it did not know him.

Do not seek God activity without seeking God. Intimacy with God should always be your motivation. He wants access to your very heart and soul. As a Father to a child, he wants you to know, love and share this life with one another. Let Him in. He's waiting.

Personal Reflection: What is God saying to Me?

Genesis 5:24 ESV

Enoch walked with God, and he was not, for God took him.

Seek God first. Spend time with Him with the intention to get up and walk with Him, following Him throughout the day. Do not simply leave God in your prayer closet. Take Him with you.

Personal Reflection: What is God saying to Me?

Isaiah 29:13 ESV

And the Lord said: "Because this people draw near with their mouth and honor me with their lips, while their hearts are far from me, and their fear of me is a commandment taught by men

Satan loves a religious Christian that is more focused on activity than God. Ask yourself today do you want Jesus? Does your daily life reflect that you want to be in relationship with Jesus and the will of the Father to be done in your life? Begin to view Jesus as the blessing.

Personal Reflection: What is God saying to Me?

Day 325

Psalm 34:18 ESV

The Lord is near to the brokenhearted and saves the crushed in spirit.

God doesn't want you to live rejected in despair. He did not die on the cross for you to live a life of misery. Give that life to Jesus. He can liberate you, heal you, restore you. All is not hopeless. That's the devil. Let God show you how to live a life of joy, peace and rest.

Personal Reflection: What is God saying to Me?

Day 326 Halloween

Ephesians 5:11 NIV

11 Have nothing to do with the fruitless deeds of darkness, but rather expose them.

What are your thoughts on Christians celebrating Halloween?

1- Harmless. All in good fun. Enjoy.

2- Satanic. Stay away at all cost. Pray.

3- Some activities are ok. Some not. Use discernment.

NEVER honor and celebrate death, darkness and evil. Pray for the souls of men.

Personal Reflection: What is God saying to Me?

Day 327

Ephesians 3:20 ASV

Now unto him that is able to do exceeding abundantly above all that we ask or think, according to the power that worketh in us.

Do you believe that you can do a better job than God with your life? Let the I AM that I AM, who orchestrated the entire universe and constructed the complexity of the human body take a crack at your life. Let Him surprise you. He does not disappoint.

Personal Reflection: What is God saying to Me?

Ephesians 3:20-21 TPT

Never doubt God's mighty power to work in you and accomplish all this. He will achieve infinitely more than your greatest request, your most unbelievable dream, and exceed your wildest imagination! He will outdo them all, for his miraculous power constantly energizes you.

Don't just imagine what it would be like to step out of the boat. Decide to LIVE walking on the water. Sure, the ones in the boat may be comfortable and in false security but you will be doing what eyes have not seen and ears have not heard. Go.

Personal Reflection: What is God saying to Me?

Hebrews 11:1 NLV

11 Now faith is being sure we will get what we hope for. It is being sure of what we cannot see.

God is asking you to make a faith decision. You won't because you do not have the resources. This is EXACTLY why He wants you to make it so that you must rely on Him to meet your needs according to His riches and glory. Make the hard decision. He's got you.

Personal Reflection: What is God saying to Me?

Matthew 14:28-30 NIV

28 "Lord, if it's you," Peter replied, "tell me to come to you on the water."m29 "Come," he said. Then Peter got down out of the boat, walked on the water and came toward Jesus. 30 But when he saw the wind, he was afraid and, beginning to sink, cried out, "Lord, save me!"

You've gotten out of the boat. Know that the challenge comes in when the comfort of the boat goes away. Trust that the one who called you out will not let you drown. He will teach you how to live on water.

Personal Reflection: What is God saying to Me?

2 Corinthians 5:17 ESV

Therefore, if anyone is in Christ, he is a new creation. The old has passed away; behold, the new has come.

Finish the statement. You know you are following God when...

I'll start. You know your following God when your "friends" start dropping off like flies.

Personal Reflection: What is God saying to Me?

1 John 5:4-5 ESV

For everyone who has been born of God overcomes the world. And this is the victory that has overcome the world—our faith. Who is it that overcomes the world except the one who believes that Jesus is the Son of God?

Be aware. Your decision to know God will also be a decision to know Satan. As God finds new ways to reveal Himself, Satan will also be revealing Himself in ways unknown before. Be ready for the encounter. Resist and He will flee.

Personal Reflection: What is God saying to Me?

Day 333

Ephesians 6:10 ESV

Finally, be strong in the Lord and in the strength of his might.

Know your enemy. What tactic does Satan use to get you to quit, run, triggers you?

1- Offense

2- Fatigue

3- heaviness, depression

4- boredom

5- overwhelmed

His strategy doesn't change. The only way to win is to know you are in a battle. Learn your enemy. Fight back in the strength of the Lord!

Personal Reflection: What is God saying to Me?

DAY 334

John 14:15 ESV

"If you love me, you will keep my commandments.

I am not exempt from this process. I am still in the midst of making hard faith decisions. In these moments, I ask myself, 'welp, I am crucified with Christ or not'. Does it get easier? No. But the more you fall in love with the Father and His Son, you know you MUST obey.

Personal Reflection: What is God saying to Me?

Luke 6:46 ESV

"Why do you call me 'Lord, Lord,' and not do what I tell you?

Why are you asking God for the next step when you haven't completed the step you are on? Step in front of you. God is not going to do all the work Himself. He wants to know what you got on it. Put your faith on it and know faith without works is dead. Go to work. He will bless it.

Personal Reflection: What is God saying to Me?

Isaiah 54:17 NKJV

17 No weapon formed against you shall prosper,

The devil should have stopped long ago or slowed down. But since He wouldn't let up and came for me relentlessly with everything he had in every aspect of my life, he showed me his hand. Now I'm mad. He pushed me right into the arms of the Father and I'm taking back everything.

Personal Reflection: What is God saying to Me?

John 21:22 ESV

Jesus said to him, "If it is my will that he remain until I come, what is that to you? You follow me!"

Stay in your lane. What has God called you to do? Do that only. Don't be where God isn't. Be where the grace is. Move in the area which you have been anointed. Don't be led by the current of the world doing any and everything. It could be a trap. Be led of God. Follow God.

Personal Reflection: What is God saying to Me?

Day 338

Psalm 28:7 ESV

The Lord is my strength and my shield; in him my heart trusts, and I am helped; my heart exults, and with my song I give thanks to him.

What keeps you from losing your life to God?

1- Lack of Faith

2- Comfort

3- Fear

4- Uncertainty

5- Lack of Trust

Bring it before the Lord and ask Him for help in this area. He wants your weakness so that He may show Himself strong in your life.

Personal Reflection: What is God saying to Me?

Colossians 3:23-24 ESV

Whatever you do, work heartily, as for the Lord and not for men, knowing that from the Lord you will receive the inheritance as your reward. You are serving the Lord Christ.

Has God called you to write a book, start a business, organize a ministry? You may not see yourself as an author, business owner or minister, but God has called you to it and will grace you to do it. Start today! Put those hands to work and give Him something to bless!

Personal Reflection: What is God saying to Me?

Galatians 2:19-21 MSG

19-21 What actually took place is this: I tried keeping rules and working my head off to please God, and it didn't work. So I quit being a "law man" so that I could be God's man. Christ's life showed me how, and enabled me to do it. I identified myself completely with him. Indeed, I have been crucified with Christ. My ego is no longer central. It is no longer important that I appear righteous before you or have your good opinion, and I am no longer driven to impress God. Christ lives in me. The life you see me living is not "mine," but it is lived by faith in the Son of God, who loved me and gave himself for me. I am not going to go back on that.

21 Is it not clear to you that to go back to that old rule-keeping, peer-pleasing religion would be an abandonment of everything personal and free in my relationship with God? I refuse to do that, to repudiate God's grace. If a living relationship with God could come by rule-keeping, then Christ died unnecessarily.

Be who you really are in Christ! God does not want to use a false representation of yourself. No. He wants the real, delivered you to go after real people who are in need of deliverance. Drop the façade and follow God.

Personal Reflection: What is God saying to Me?

James 1:5 NIV

If any of you lacks wisdom, you should ask God, who gives generously to all without finding fault, and it will be given to you.

Use discernment. Ask God about the people and situations you encounter. They could be sent by the enemy to drain you of your resources. God knows your heart and so does the devil. Proceed with caution!

Personal Reflection: What is God saying to Me?

Matthew 25:21 ESV

His master said to him, 'Well done, good and faithful servant. You have been faithful over a little; I will set you over much. Enter into the joy of your master.'

Do not consider the opinions of others in the decision to Follow God. They will not be with you after your time here has expired. Long to here, job well down. Dare to abandon all reason and go into the deep with Him. He's waiting.

Personal Reflection: What is God saying to Me?

Day 343

Psalms 25:1 NLT

O LORD, I give my life to you. I trust in you, my God! Do not let me be disgraced, or let my enemies rejoice in my defeat. No one who trusts in you will ever be disgraced, but disgrace comes to those who try to deceive others.

What is your response? Tell the truth, shame the devil.

I am 100% sold out to Christ

1- Yes

2- No

3- I'm getting there

4- Not interested

What is it that stops you from being 100% sold out to Christ? Whatever it is, it is not worth the glory of the Lord. Give it over to God and watch God do the unimaginable thing in your life.

Personal Reflection: What is God saying to Me?

John 10:10 ESV

The thief comes only to steal and kill and destroy. I came that they may have life and have it abundantly.

Let the Lord upgrade you! Do you think your life is going to get worse? No, He offers abundant life. It is the devil that kills, steals and destroys. Come out of agreement with the devil, enter into covenant with God and let Him walk you into your promise land.

Personal Reflection: What is God saying to Me?

Galatians 5:7 NLT

7 You were running the race so well. Who has held you back from following the truth?

You were running the race so well. Who has held you back from following the truth? Does someone come to mind? Bring them before the Lord. Ask for the next step.

Personal Reflection: What is God saying to Me?

1 Corinthians 9:22 NIV

To the weak I became weak, to win the weak. I have become all things to all people so that by all possible means I might save some.

I asked the Lord, what is the limit in becoming all things to save souls and God's response was that that was the limit-to do it to save souls. Once you do it to satisfy the flesh and you have come under the power of it, it needs to be surrendered to God. Stay free. Stay God's.

Personal Reflection: What is God saying to Me?

Matthew 27:45-46; 50 NLT

45 At noon, darkness fell across the whole land until three o'clock.
46 At about three o'clock, Jesus called out with a loud voice, "Eli,
Eli,[a] lema sabachthani?" which means "My God, my God, why
have you abandoned me?"

50 Then Jesus shouted out again, and he released his spirit.

No gimmicks. No slogans. No themes. Only God. Follow Him.
Live for Him. Take up your cross and go away with Him.

Personal Reflection: What is God saying to Me?

1 Kings 18:21 ESV

And Elijah came near to all the people and said, "How long will you go limping between two different opinions? If the Lord is God, follow him; but if Baal, then follow him." And the people did not answer him a word.

Today, the Lord had me make a right now message to His people. Choose this day whom you will serve, make a decision. The Lord is not playing and is requiring you to give Him all of you. He is in need of you. The time is now. Jesus is coming back. Make your decision.

Personal Reflection: What is God saying to Me?

Matthew 19:29 NIV

And everyone who has left houses or brothers or sisters or father or mother or wife or children or fields for my sake will receive a hundred times as much and will inherit eternal life.

What could Satan offer you for your soul? What is your soul-your mind, will, emotions, imaginations, reasonings and intellect. Do you know God wants your whole soul? Why won't you give it to Him. Don't you see? Thats what Satan has given you for your soul. He already has it.

Personal Reflection: What is God saying to Me?

Ecclesiastes 3:11 ESV

He has made everything beautiful in its time. Also, he has put eternity into man's heart, yet so that he cannot find out what God has done from the beginning to the end.

Three types of Christians: 1) Christlike- Job. Blameless- a man of integrity. Feared God, stayed away from evil. 2) Followers of Christ- Abraham- What God instructed Abraham to do, He did. 3) Slaves and Prisoners of Christ- Paul, Jesus. I move as God leads. What type are you?

Personal Reflection: What is God saying to Me?

John 8:12 ESV

Again Jesus spoke to them, saying, "I am the light of the world. Whoever follows me will not walk in darkness, but will have the light of life."

Who you following? I pray it's Jesus.

Personal Reflection: What is God saying to Me?

Proverbs 19:21 ESV

Many are the plans in the mind of a man, but it is the purpose of the Lord that will stand.

What is the message? Follow God. God has a great plan for you. You don't have to figure life out. You don't have to go through life not knowing who you are. Don't guess at life. Don't rely on others, the internet or the world. Go to God, surrender and follow Him. He's waiting.

Personal Reflection: What is God saying to Me?

Psalm 90:17 ESV

Let the favor of the Lord our God be upon us, and establish the work of our hands upon us; yes, establish the work of our hands!

The Lord is teaching me in this season about the relationship between working with your hands and trusting God. There is work that we need to do to prepare, perform and promote but there is also a knowing that God is in the midst of all that and you are not alone. Work hard and leave the rest to God.

Personal Reflection: What is God saying to Me?

John 15:15 NIV

15 I no longer call you servants, because a servant does not know his master's business. Instead, I have called you friends, for everything that I learned from my Father I have made known to you.

Do you have a friend? So many people are alone for many different reasons. You may have felt rejected, or been harmed? The devil may have caused you to isolate, or God has asked you to remove people. Know you are never alone. Let God be your companion and cling to Him with everything you have.

Personal Reflection: What is God saying to Me?

Day 355

1 Corinthians 6:12 AMP

Everything is permissible for me, but not all things are beneficial. Everything is permissible for me, but I will not be enslaved by anything [and brought under its power, allowing it to control me].

What are you addicted to? See, we think drugs, sex, alcohol but we need to consider social media, exercise or health and fitness, shopping. 1 COR 6:12 "I am allowed to do anything"—but ... I must not become a slave to anything." Give addictions over to God. He will make a way.

Personal Reflection: What is God saying to Me?

DAY 356

1 Timothy 4:8 ASV

For bodily exercise is profitable for a little; but godliness is profitable for all things, having promise of the life which now is, and of that which is to come.

Fitness enthusiasts reconsider your idea of fitness. It is not about what you can do in the gym, it is how you live your life. Are you healthy, strong, vibrant, full of energy, ready and available to conquer the things of God or are you broken down in a constant state of recovery? If it is an idol, give it over to God.

Personal Reflection: What is God saying to Me?

Day 357

Luke 12:48 DARBY

And to every one to whom much has been given, much shall be required from him; and to whom [men] have committed much, they will ask from him the more.

About me. About you. I am a retired military construction worker of 20 years. I have a master's degree from fuller theological seminary. I have run two marathons. I have traveled the world and done much more. God allowed me to exhaust life so He could have it and now I am available as God leads to serve you. God maybe allowing you to exhaust life but know there is an appointed time for all. When the time comes will you be willing to give Him all of you?

Personal Reflection: What is God saying to Me?

Day 358

Psalm 73:25-26

Whom have I in heaven but you? And there is nothing on earth that I desire besides you. My flesh and my heart may fail, but God is the strength of my heart and my portion forever.

Ok, so what do you need for a fresh start? Do you need to fast, stop an addiction? Forgive? Confess and repent? Make sure whatever needs to happen to have a fresh start you don't think twice about it and simply do it. Nothing is worth your mind renewal and the purity of your connection with God.

Personal Reflection: What is God saying to Me?

Day 359

Romans 8:5 ESV

For those who live according to the flesh set their minds on the things of the flesh, but those who live according to the Spirit set their minds on the things of the Spirit.

We are supposed to walk with God. God will instruct you. He will lead you. Those that are led of the spirit are children of God. God still speaks to His children as He did with Moses, Abraham, Jeremiah. As Jesus spoke with Paul so He shall speak with you. Give Him your time and your whole life. He's waiting.

Personal Reflection: What is God saying to Me?

Day 360

John 15:18 NIV

18 "If the world hates you, keep in mind that it hated me first.

Jesus did not have it easy during His ministry. Often, we look at difficulty, hardship or challenge in ministry as an indication to quit but it is a part of it. Jesus was laughed at, mocked, set up, accused of the worse, doubted and crucified. They will hate you and come against you just as they did Jesus. Cling to Him.

Personal Reflection: What is God saying to Me?

Isaiah 43:18 NIV

"Forget the former things; do not dwell on the past.

Let go. Surrender. Make room. Isaiah 43:18-19 "Forget the former things; do not dwell on the past. See, I am doing a new thing! Now it springs up; do you not perceive it?" You must let go of the past, the old, to receive the new. Let go of the you you know and the life your use to and let God reveal the true you and walk you into new life.

Personal Reflection: What is God saying to Me?

Mark 3:5 NASB

After looking around at them with anger, grieved at their hardness of heart, He *said to the man, "Stretch out your hand." And he stretched it out, and his hand was restored.

The Lord spoke to me about stretching. He reminded me to stay in it. Nothing changes if nothing changes. Lean into the stretch don't run from it and the change you have prayed your whole life for will happen. Give it chance.

Personal Reflection: What is God saying to Me?

Galatians 1 :1-2 NIV

1Paul, an apostle—sent not from men nor by a man, but by Jesus Christ and God the Father, who raised him from the dead— 2and all the brothers and sisters with me,

Adopt the mind of Paul. Man did not send me, Jesus did. Not my own revelation but Christ. I did not come to please man or get His approval only Christ. In the end it, we must hear job well done not from man but Christ.

Personal Reflection: What is God saying to Me?

Day 364

Genesis 3:1 MSG

1The serpent was clever, more clever than any wild animal God had made. He spoke to the Woman: "Do I understand that God told you not to eat from any tree in the garden?"

God told me to "keep going. Don't rely on feelings and emotions- the devil is working through them. Get up every morning, deny yourself and do what I have instructed you to do." Don't believe the lies of the enemy. Push past them and do what God has called you to do.

Personal Reflection: What is God saying to Me?

Galatians 2:19-21 MSG

Indeed, I have been crucified with Christ.

Do you want to be crucified with Christ? Know what that means: total and complete. Will you kill all attachment, wants, desires even needs? Will you lose your life to Jesus? This is what He requires. Deny yourself, crucify yourself, follow Him.

LETTER FROM GOD

Congratulations! You have completed the 365-day devotional book. Whether you have only read one day of the devotional, many days or all of it, know that I am proud of you. I am proud that you cared enough about your walk with Me to purchase a book to help you grow in your faith, opened it up and read it. Continue seeking Me and searching to connect with Me in new and diverse ways.

I love you child. I love that you want to spend time with me and develop our relationship. I want to spend time with you too. Reading hours of scripture and prayer are not required; just, your earnest desire to meet with Me and I will meet with you wherever you are.

Let's this book be only one step of many in our journey together. I led you to this devotional. Seek Me and listen for the next step. We have been through much together- more than you will ever know. We still have much more to do and I have so much more I want to show you if you will partner with Me and allow me too. What is required of you? What will it cost you?

Everything.

. . .

Will you pay the cost? Know, my child, whether you will or not, I will always love you and the option remains on the table. When you are ready to come to me, then go away with Me.

Matthew 11:28-30 MSG

"Are you tired? Worn out? Burned out on religion? Come to me. Get away with me and you'll recover your life. I'll show you how to take a real rest. Walk with me and work with me—watch how I do it. Learn the unforced rhythms of grace. I won't lay anything heavy or ill-fitting on you. Keep company with me and you'll learn to live freely and lightly."

The decision is yours.